MISS HOWARD
AND THE EMPEROR

Miss Howard in 1850

Simone André Maurois

MISS HOWARD
AND
THE EMPEROR

Translated from the French by
Humphrey Hare

NEW YORK
ALFRED A. KNOPF

Published January 13, 1958

Second Printing, February 1958

Third Printing, March 1958

MANUFACTURED IN THE UNITED STATES OF AMERICA

To André Maurois

ACKNOWLEDGMENTS

I AM grateful to Commandant de Fréminville, who has been kind enough to permit me to reproduce the portrait of his great-grandmother and has lent me the albums of his grandfather, the Comte de Béchevêt. I am no less grateful to Mme G. Ratisbonne de Ravenel, great-granddaughter of the Comtesse de Beauregard, who has placed family material at my disposal. Without their generous kindness this book would be incomplete.

Maître Jacques Mahot de La Quérantonnais is the great-grandson of, and direct successor, to Maître Amédée Mocquard, lawyer to the Imperial family. Mrs. Trelawny, Comtesse de Beauregard, was not only a client of the firm, but a friend of Maître Mocquard, of his sister Camille, of his father, Jean, *chef de cabinet* to Napoleon III, and of his stepmother (*née* Marie-Alida Gounon). Maître Mahot de La Quérantonnais has kindly permitted me to consult his great-grand-father's archives. There is such an abundance of documents in this collection that selection has been my main difficulty.

I owe to Mr. Ivor Guest, the author of an admirable work, *Napoleon III in England*, unpublished information and important references. He has communicated to me a great quantity of information drawn from his own papers; I wish to express to him my gratitude, as I do to Miss Reardon of the Harvard Theatrical Collection, U.S.A., and to the founders of the Raymond Mander and Joe Mitchenson Theatre Collection, London. My thanks are also due to Mrs. Grinling, Prince Jean-Louis de Faucigny-Lucinge and to Mme Guy Dorget. Our friend Jacques Suffel has greatly assisted my researches in the Bibliothèque Nationale.

Mrs. Joan St. George Saunders and Mrs. Philip Astley, founders of *Writer's and Speaker's Research* in London, have placed the great resources of their organisation at my disposal. It is impossible to exaggerate the admirable services they render those who, unable to

7

live in England, nevertheless need to make researches there. For example, the facts I am able to publish to-day upon the origin of Miss Howard and upon the identity of her son are the result of Mrs. Saunders's patient examination of the parish registers of many churches spread over several counties. *Writer's and Speaker's Research* have also found for me certain works which were out of print and appeared to be unprocurable.

My grateful thanks are also due to M. Émile Pelletier, Préfet de La Seine, who granted me free access to the domain of Beauregard which is at present closed to the public, and to M. Robert Joffet, *Conservateur des Parcs, Jardins et Espaces Verts*, through whose good offices I have been enabled to visit the little room at Bagatelle in which both Lord Hertford and his only son, Sir Richard Wallace, died.

A list of works consulted is printed at the end of the book.

S. A. M.

CONTENTS

9

ILLUSTRATIONS

THE CHÂTEAU DE BEAUREGARD

A few miles from Paris there is a mysterious region enclosed within high walls. It is the ancient seigneurial fief of Beauregard. Its woodlands occupy an area of approximately five hundred acres between La Celle-Saint-Cloud, Rocquencourt and Marly-le-Roi. What was once a splendid park is relapsing into a wilderness and within its green depths lies the spectre of a great house fallen into decay.

The motor road from the west crosses the enchanted domain. From the road itself one can see one of the five lodges attached to the five monumental iron gates. Beyond the wall, the forest is returning to its natural state. Ivy clings to the ancient trees and the landscaped paths are lost to view beneath a thick carpet of green moss.

The phantom house remains invisible amid its wild jungle. Its masters have been absent from France for half a century, and have forsaken it. Beset by wild grasses, besieged by riotous thickets, it is in process of falling victim to fifty winters of indifference and inclemency.

Beauregard, which is not listed as an ancient monument, will disappear. At the moment of writing, an individual and a public body are disputing its possession. Maurice-Arnold de Forest, Comte de Bendern, generously offered the great property to the City of Paris in 1950; to-day he wishes to reclaim it because the conditions of his gift have not been fulfilled within the stated time. But without the reprieve *in extremis* of being scheduled as an ancient monument, the château will be torn down.

With Beauregard will perish the insubstantial portrait of a woman whose memory survives only in the existence of her house. It was she who turned the ancient monastery, which had become a country house under Louis XIV, into this Second Empire Palace. It was she, too, who surrounded the park with a crenellated wall. And again it was she who, wishing to adorn the Temple of Abandon with allegories, crowned the two principal façades with sculptured groups. On the north, an unfaithful Amour is taking flight, while the fair victim from whom he tries to fly has seized him by a wing in a vain effort to detain him. On the south, the figures supporting the sundial express the idea that Love fades with Time. It is a fantastic décor, now still visible though we know it is to be destroyed; a décor conceived and erected by an actress who here played out her final scene: that of her own death.

New people, without links with those of the past, have come upon the scene. The district, they say, must be cleared of these ruins. Unanimous upon this point, they are in disagreement upon all others. The giver is opposed to the wishes of a committee organised to decide upon the future of his gift. At Beauregard, it is no longer to-day a question of resolving a sentimental intrigue, but of solving a problem of town planning. Paris, too, populous, is overflowing its limits. In a period of crisis, the survival of private woodlands in its suburbs is an intolerable anachronism. Here are to be constructed blocks of flats in a utilitarian style of architecture which collectively, so it is said, will form the XXIe arrondissement. A new town will be founded as a satellite. Thus Paris will no longer be all of a piece. Some Sunday a minister will lay the first stone of Paris *bis* (Seine-et-Oise).

I wished to see the dying house before it was razed to the ground. Built between the Seine and the Mauldre, on the northern slope of a high plateau, at the top of a narrow valley

14

which falls steeply to Bougival, it once proudly crowned the heights. It is said that from its terraces the view extended between the wooded hills of Louveciennes and of La Celle-Saint-Cloud, to the great loop of the Seine which envelops Croissy. In the distance, beyond Sannois and Eaubonne, the forest of Montmorency lay dark upon the blue horizon. But nothing of all this is to be seen to-day. In half a century, too many trees grow and multiply. The aspect of the country must be sought for in old letters where it is frequently described as " the most beautiful view in the province."

Nature, so long controlled, here takes its wild revenge. Gardeners and landscape-gardeners created on this spot a superb rose-garden, smooth lawns, an Elizabethan maze, and slopes covered with rhododendrons and azaleas. But human order yields to the anarchy of the vegetable world. Beauregard, a haunted house, is no longer defended from the irresistible pressure of root and branch. The woods encircle it and press upon it.

She, who once planned and decorated so magnificently, had a sense of mystery. She made a frame for her legend. Having built this work of stone and lived under the blazon of Beauregard, she imagined that her memory would thereby be assured against oblivion for centuries to come. But in this she was wrong.

The decaying house has taken on the mournful aspect of a violated tomb. Its walls are scarred with great wounds opening upon naked rooms. Through gaping rents in the sloping roof the rain pours in upon the cracked and rotting floors. Beauregard is crumbling and disintegrating. The light shade of its lady has fled by paths whose windings have faded and no longer lead anywhere. Once the domain is broken up into lots, what will remain of the dead, forgotten woman? What trace has she left behind her? How can one seize the form, the secret transparency of vanished beauty?

When I went to Beauregard, I knew that a foreign woman, known by the name of Miss Howard, had shut herself up in this house, having literally made an Emperor of the French. She was supposed to have been ennobled under the title of her estate by Napoleon III.

Miss Howard has her paragraph in every History of France. Her name is mentioned at least once in the chapter upon the origins of the Second Republic. Mistress of the Prince-President, we are told that she was his partner in his election campaigns; and later in his *coup d'état*. Like an actress in the limelight, she appears, brilliantly illuminated, between two zones of darkness. But this pale shooting star was unable to attach itself to the political firmament. She has left no trace upon it. We do not know what Miss Howard was, where she came from, nor what became of her. Before the haunting décor of Beauregard, the house of death, I promised myself to resolve this triple problem.

In the cemetery of Grand-Chesnay, near Rocquencourt, I discovered, under the shadow of the yews, twin tombs covered with all-devouring ivy. I read:

COMTESSE	MARTIN
DE BEAUREGARD	CONSTANTIN
née Howard	Comte de Béchevêt
(1822–1864)	(1842–1907)
Pray for her!	

At the *mairie* at La Celle-Saint-Cloud, I had the opportunity of consulting the contemporary archives. The civil register showed that Elizabeth Ann Haryett, landowner, aged 41 years, born in England, wife of Clarence Trelawny, had died on the 19th August, 1865, at her residence, the Château de Beauregard. Here no title of Comtesse adorns the defunct châtelaine who, as a girl, was called, so it appeared, Miss Haryett and not Miss Howard. I did not know that she had been married; the name of Trelawny was a revelation to me. The death certificate, which gives this disconcerting woman's date of birth as 1824, contradicted every statement made on her tombstone. Indeed, every single statement without exception, since, as well as the pseudonym and courtesy title, the two dates are false.

Harriet Howard, who called herself " Comtesse de Beauregard in France," was therefore neither Howard nor Beauregard. What is no less curious, is that Harriet, a delightful Christian name, was not the Christian name of the future Miss Howard. Except for two letters the name was her surname. Like Sidonie-Gabrielle Colette in our own day, she made a Christian name out of a surname.

Why should the rich and powerful Egeria of Napoleon III hide her identity? For what extraordinary reasons could she have wished to create uncertainty and spread obscurity? Driving back to Paris that evening, I decided to solve the Howard mystery.

I acquired a number of books which describe, nearly all briefly, her political and sentimental adventure. The scholars are content to say that Miss Howard, an extremely beautiful young Englishwoman, had lent five million gold francs (the equivalent of a million pounds sterling in 1956) to Prince Louis Napoleon Bonaparte in order that the man she loved might be elected by universal suffrage. The anti-Bonapartist pamphlets rate her very low in order to attack, through her, the man who was under an obligation to her. Those writers of memoirs who saw her in the flesh do not make her character intelligible.

Hector Fleischmann, the historian of the Second Empire, has published in facsimile[1] a certificate of baptism found by him and dated 23rd October, 1822. It is that of a child named Elizabeth Herriott whose father, Henry Herriott, was a brewer at Preston. The author strongly maintains that Elizabeth Herriott is the famous Miss Howard. But in this he is in error. I shall show that the death certificate presents the truth and that the Emperor's mistress was in fact called Elizabeth Ann Haryett. The labours of M. Fleischmann inspired a certain confident temerity in other writers, and they continued to confuse, as he had done, the two

---

[1] In *Napoléon III et les femmes, d'après les mémoires des contemporains, les pamphlets, les journaux satiriques, des documents nouveaux et inedits*, p. 152-3.

contemporary Elizabeths on the grounds of a single common Christian name.

In 1938 Adrien Dansette, an excellent and scrupulous historian, still believed (because he followed Fleischmann's lead) that Miss Howard " was the daughter of a Sussex brewer named Herriot." [1] In a book, published thirty-five years after Fleischmann's, Léon Treich gives Miss Howard her true name, but writes: " Elizabeth Ann Haryett was born at Dover, in May 1823 ... Her father was a boatman on the Thames; her mother a little sempstress in the most modest way of business ... She herself, at the age of sixteen, was a servant in an ill-frequented public house in the suburbs ..." [2]

Researches undertaken not only in France but in England, and pursued with some tenacity, permit us to assert to-day that Miss Howard was born neither at Preston nor at Dover. Her father, Joseph Gawen Haryett, was no more a brewer than he was a Thames boatman. Moreover, at sixteen, the supposed barmaid was an actress appearing at the Haymarket Theatre in London. No one has established this till now.

I propose to tell of the exotic, eccentric and wasted life of Elizabeth Ann Haryett, called Howard.

[1] Adrien Dansette, *Les Amours de Napoléon III*, p. 65.
[2] Léon Treich, *Les Alcôves de Napoléon III*, p. 49.

CHAPTER ONE

LITTLE BESS

BRIGHTON HAD, at this time, already become a fashionable seaside resort in full process of development. George IV had made it the mode. When the King was still no more than a prodigal and loose-living Prince Regent, he had had built for himself a strange palace there in the Oriental style. The Castle Hotel, close to the Pavilion, and passing at that time for one of the best hotels in the town, prospered.

It was at Brighton that, in a little house, No. 43 King Street, Gerrard's Court, Elizabeth Ann was born of the marriage of Joseph Gawen Haryett and Elizabeth Alderton. The grandfather of the child was the proprietor of the Castle Hotel; her father, a bootmaker, provided footwear for the fashionable ladies; her mother did not go out to work.

At that period, there were no registers kept in Town Halls and the Crown authorities relied upon the Established Church. The entry in the Parish Register was equivalent to a birth certificate. The first documentation of Elizabeth Ann's life is, therefore, to be found in the Parish Church of St. Nicholas. She was baptised there according to the rites of the Church of England on the 13th August, 1823. From which it can be determined that, if her epitaph ages her by one year, her death certificate makes her younger by a similar period.

Upon the early youth of Miss Howard we have but a single witness: herself. Her unpublished correspondence contains no reference that can help us to determine why the Haryett family

19

left Brighton, a gay and charming town, in order to establish itself farther north, at Great Yarmouth in Norfolk. Nor does the writer tell us at what period of her childhood this migration took place. Perhaps the hotel business had sufficiently enriched her grandfather to enable him to retire from business and buy a country house and estate for his children. However that may be, the fact of Joseph Haryett's property cannot be doubted since, in his old age, we find him designated from time to time as either "landowner" or "gentleman" in a number of authentic documents. He became, indeed, Joseph Gawen Haryett, Esquire.

In Norfolk, where she was brought up, Elizabeth—whom everyone called Little Bess, in order to distinguish her from her mother—learned to ride. She quickly became an accomplished horsewoman. Mr. Haryett, a churchman of strict principles, was dumbfounded to discover that he had fathered a daughter who was not only dangerously beautiful and a great reader of novels, but rode too hard at her fences.

Mrs. Haryett, as faithful a churchgoer as her husband, organised a village workroom where her neighbours came to sew and knit for the county poor. Little Bess, having been enrolled, plied her needle in such a desultory way, that her mother ordered her to read the Bible aloud during the hours of work rather than spend the time day-dreaming. Since the young Elizabeth possessed an illustrated edition of *The Plays of Shakespeare*, she suggested to her audience that she might from time to time add a few extracts from these celebrated tragedies to the reading of Holy Writ. Shakespeare being a classic author, and the edition wisely expurgated, the Christian women saw no harm in it. Nevertheless, the devil had taken on the mask of Shakespeare to tempt Miss Haryett and she was lost.

A real and growing enthusiasm possessed her. Passionately devoted to poetry, she learned whole poems by heart. An irresistible vocation became evident. At Juliet's age, Little Bess told her horrified parents that she wished to become a great actress! Mr. and Mrs. Haryett were aghast; their stupefaction was succeeded by indignation. The members of the workroom shared their horror. The whole parish was upset.

The violence of the reaction itself aroused in Elizabeth Ann a determination to run away. Unsuited to country life, she regretted the gaiety of Brighton and dreamed of the wonders of the capital. A passion for Shakespeare was therefore the operative impulse in removing this girl, still so young, from her family and drawing her to the stage, upon which she dreamed of playing Juliet, Ophelia, Ariel and, Desdemona.

Joseph and Elizabeth Haryett " had no wish to have an actress for a daughter." Their opposition to a project that they qualified as " scandalous " was immovable. Little Bess, who felt she was being treated harshly, found sympathy from her " dear Aunt Frances " (Mrs. Charles Alderton), a kindly woman who, unlike her brother-in-law and sister-in-law, did not live in an unhealthy fear of sin. Alfred and Thomas Alderton, Elizabeth Ann's cousins, chivalrously took the part of their pretty, persecuted relation.

But the privileges of a father—at that period all-powerful and absolute—gave Joseph Haryett the right to prevent his daughter, who was still a minor, from going upon the stage, even if he had to place her under restraint. Elizabeth Haryett was too submissive a wife to take upon herself the defence of her daughter against the wishes of her lord and master. " What could I do to escape from so old-fashioned a family," wrote Elizabeth Ann, " what could I do but run away ? "

At this moment, an old client from the Castle Hotel at Brighton, accompanied by his son aged twenty-three, visited the district. The father was called Thomas Mason. He was a horse-coper from Stilton in Huntingdonshire who had made a fortune out of dealing in bloodstock. The son, whose name was James,[1]

---

[1] He was baptised on the 13th January, 1816, at Stilton. Later he lived at Woodhall, near Pinner, and in Oxford Street in London, in a house upon the present site of Marble Arch. Having been twice married, he died of consumption on the 23rd October, 1866.

nicknamed Jem, rode steeplechases and had won the Grand National in 1839. As a boy he had done well at the Huntingdon Grammar School. A brilliant horseman, he is still known to-day as " the most famous steeplechase rider of all time."

The Masons, father and son, whom business connected with horses had taken to Norfolk, stayed there for some time. They paid a visit to the Haryett family. Jem, at Brighton, had known Little Bess at an ungrateful age. When he saw her again, he was entranced. At fifteen, having lost none of her childish grace, she had acquired the subtle art of attracting men. Though they did not all fall in love with her, there was none who was not enchanted. Jem Mason, though merely a visitor, was the recipient of her unhappy, touching confidences. Elizabeth Ann told him of her difficulties with her father. By what right did this narrow-minded tyrant " stifle the budding rose, prevent its bursting into flower "? A great artist wished to go upon the London stage but her father wished to marry her off, and would have given her away to any Tom, Dick or Harry in the neighbourhood. Jem was taken into the girl's confidence; she asked his advice. Could not the district do with a housewife the less, and Shakespeare with an interpreter the more?

The jockey, who was also an ardent rider to hounds, was no less an amateur of the theatre. He had contacts in greenrooms and with managers. When Little Bess confided her unhappiness to him, he offered to take her to London and help her (in the most honourable manner in the world) to get an opening in the theatre.

The result of this promise was exactly what follows from all promises men make in similar cases. Miss Haryett made the journey to London at the cost of her virtue. She thought she had found a chivalrous friend: she had merely found an enterprising Lovelace.

Little Bess's parents were shocked by her flight. For many months, they tried to save their face by saying that Elizabeth

Ann, wishing to educate herself, had accepted a post near Cambridge as riding-mistress in a girl's school where, in exchange for the lessons she gave, she would be instructed in letters and manners. All relations ceased between the puritan parents and the prodigal child. The break was permanent.

In London Miss Haryett, having broken with her family, called herself an orphan and took the name of Howard. Hoping for fame, the sixteen-year-old actress achieved her first part at the Haymarket Theatre, on the 16th January, 1840, in a comedy by Sheridan Knowles[1] called *The Love Chase*. The play had had a great success three years earlier. The creator of the part of Constance, having signed a contract elsewhere, was succeeded by Miss Howard. But Drury Lane, the theatre of theatres, remained the supreme goal of her aspirations.

There was no question of playing Juliet. Of only mediocre talent, Harriet Howard never succeeded in playing important parts. As a beginner, her great beauty militated against her eventual success. She suffered the misfortune of a new actress who attracts attention without later being able to justify it. The public, happily surprised in the first instance, demands that an actress shall be able to live up to its first admiring reaction. Beauty does not pay on the stage.

Throughout 1840 and 1841 she had setback after setback and disappointment after disappointment. In the theatre, Miss Howard received but the smallest parts. She lived luxuriously with Jem Mason at 277 Oxford Street, but she was unhappy in their irregular union. Jem, having seduced her, refused to marry her. He was an unscrupulous libertine, a cynic without illusions. Consumptive, he burnt up his days, pursuing every will-o'-the-wisp. A gambler, he bet on horses and played high in gaming houses. He had made a kept woman of an ingenuous, confiding country girl.

Though without talent, Miss Howard nevertheless persevered

---

[1] James Sheridan Knowles (1784-1862), dramatic author; a near relation of the great Sheridan.

in the career she had chosen. This was partly due to the fact that she believed herself fit to perform and compete; but more perhaps because she wished to justify the luxury in which she lived by exercising a recognised profession. Little Bess blushed to think herself a lost woman.

Jem Mason was not himself well born, but he knew many men who were and introduced them to his mistress. Fashionably dressed, she was " soon famous for her carriage-horses and her establishment, and was much admired in the park and in the hunting-field as the most brilliant of horsewomen. She played an exceptional part in that conventional world known as ' the high fashion.' " [1] Miss Howard's beauty gave Jem Mason a certain prestige, but he did not love her and she had never loved him.

Then once again the devil was made man.

*   *   *

Francis Mountjoy Martyn, a major in the 2nd Life Guards, was a brilliant officer of good family.[2] Born in 1809, he had spent his childhood in India where his father, Charles Fuller Martyn, a servant of the East India Company, was Sheriff of Calcutta. Then, as was the custom, he had been educated at Eton. From there, without going to the University, he had, at eighteen, been commissioned direct into the army as a cornet.

Upon the death of various relations he had become possessed of a huge fortune. All fortunes impose the obligation of producing an heir and Mountjoy Martyn had married young, less from thoughtless inclination than in order to found a numerous family. At Beachley Court in Gloucestershire, he had found, courted, and married an admirable young woman called Amelia

---

[1] cf. Comte Fleury and Louis Sonolet, *La Société du Second Empire*, Vol. I, p. 10-11.

[2] Francis Mountjoy Martyn, born in 1809, was commissioned in the Life Guards on the 27th December, 1827. Promoted colonel in 1857, he sent in his papers soon afterwards. He died in London at 17 Charles Street, Berkeley Square, on the 24th January, 1874.

Jenkins. Miss Jenkins's evident virtues, her seriousness and her delicacy, had formed the basis of the suitor's choice; but these very qualities were boring to a husband.

Shy and reserved, she was ill-equipped to hold an active, energetic man, born of much travelled parents and himself full of the zest of living. A number of accidents in pregnancy having destroyed Amelia's feeble health, her boisterous husband had detached himself from a companion who was always ailing or convalescent. She lived in retirement in the country. He went to see her, on occasion.

In 1841 Major Martyn met the dark-haired beauty. He was thirty-two years old; she was eighteen. There are numerous, and extraordinarily unanimous witnesses to the radiant beauty of Miss Howard at that time. She was described by one of her countrymen in these terms: " An exquisite apparition, full of grace and dignity. A face worthy to inspire the sculptors of ancient Greece . . ." And a French admirer: " The head of an antique cameo placed upon a superb body; a lively intelligence and a most brilliant horsewoman . . . Beautiful clothes, exquisite turnouts and a luxurious house . . ."

The ardent major desired to make this desirable conquest. He had no difficulty in convincing the ravishing actress that Jem Mason was an unworthy protector and that the " horse-coper " degraded her. Miss Howard should break with him and, that done, should swear fidelity to the major who was so smitten with her charms. Mountjoy Martyn offered a stable " arrangement " which, he said, would have all the appearance of marriage. As she could not be his legitimate wife, Harriet would be " his hostess," publicly acknowledged. He would give her a fine house: Rockingham House, St. John's Wood. Was not this verdant district the most agreeable in all London? Many painters dwelt there. And there Miss Howard might entertain to dinner all Mountjoy Martyn's friends. Together they would give balls and musical evenings at Rockingham House.

Miss Howard was tempted. Francis made a splendid-looking

soldier in his fine Life Guards' uniform. They had mutual tastes: they both loved horses, dancing, hunting and the theatre. In short, she accepted.

The major immediately made generous and provident dispositions in her favour. He placed a capital sum to be administered by trustees, of which Miss Howard was to enjoy the income during the whole of her life, though without being able to dispose of the capital. The young woman's fortune was always to be subject to reinvestment. This was a clause designed to defend her against herself and to put her under the care of persons, as financial advisers, who could best suggest profitable investments. Miss Howard agreed. The contract was signed, as if it were a marriage settlement. Francis Mountjoy Martyn, the undivorced husband of Amelia Jenkins, was taking a second wife outside marriage but with similar financial arrangements.

Jem Mason, the horse-coper, was naturally sent back to his beloved stables.

In 1842 the Theatre Royal, Drury Lane, put on *Macbeth*, which requires a numerous cast. In order to complete it, extras were engaged. This was an unhoped for opportunity for Harriet; once a member of this superior company, she would know how to retain her place. She happily accepted the part of the Third Apparition in Act IV, wearing a crown on her head and bearing a tree in her hand.

The part has only one speech both famous and prophetic:

> Be lion-mettled, proud, and take no care
> Who chafes, who frets, or where conspirers are;
> Macbeth shall never vanquish'd be until
> Great Birnam wood to high Dunsinane hill
> Shall come against him.

That night Miss Howard, divinely Shakespearian in the closed sovereign crown of the Kings of Scotland, did not go unremarked. There was applause in the auditorium. But when *Macbeth* was played again at Drury Lane, the name of Harriet Howard had disappeared from the bill. The Third Apparition had been pregnant for several months.

On the 16th August, 1842, she gave birth to a son by Major Mountjoy Martyn. The child, unfortunately illegitimate, had only the right to his mother's name. He was called Martin Constantine Haryett. Brought up a Protestant by churchgoing parents, the mother wished to make of her son a good Anglican. The 27th September was chosen for his baptism.

The idea of going to the parish priest, the Reverend Arthur Baker, with an illegitimate child by an unknown father, was intolerable to Miss Howard. The rebellious daughter of conforming parents, she had braved the family code in order to go upon the stage, but her puritanical heredity came to the fore when it was a question of her own child. How could she permit the innocent infant to become an object of scandal? Miss Haryett, alias Howard, had courageously accepted her responsibilities as an unmarried mother. Nevertheless, she could not bear the thought that, because of his illegitimacy, society would hold Martin in contempt. She would go to all lengths to efface this basic misfortune. She was prepared to dare all.

She decided to lie. Mrs. Joseph Haryett was less than forty years old; it was quite possible that she might still give birth to a last child. Living far off, she would never discover the plot invented by Elizabeth Ann, her guilty daughter, whose good name was tarnished. Miss Howard therefore presented for baptism in Trinity Church, Marylebone, a child who was said to have been born of the marriage of Joseph Gawen Haryett and Elizabeth Alderton. Herself the daughter of this union, Elizabeth Ann passed herself off as the elder sister of her son, whom she held at the font.

She was that day as simply dressed as any young woman in modest circumstances, since it was important that the christening should pass unnoticed. At the moment when the baptismal certificate—which was, indeed, a falsification of a public document—was copied into the parish register, the godmother was asked the profession of Mr. Haryett, the father of the child. She casually replied: " Plumber."

The legitimate and pitiful Mrs. Francis Mountjoy Martyn no longer had any hope of becoming a mother. The doctors had not concealed from the major that his broken marriage, which henceforth was motiveless, would always be sterile. Nevertheless, he suffered from a frequently expressed regret, that which Freud in the twentieth century has called a paternity complex. He wished to assure the future of his illegitimate son.

English law at that time was pitiless to illegitimate children. In order not to attract attention, it was better not to indulge in a legacy which might be suspect. But it was quite proper for a rich man during his lifetime to make gift upon gift to a mistress. Having given Major Martyn a son, Miss Howard received in exchange a considerable fortune. The illegitimate heir was born with a silver spoon in his mouth.

Harriet's trick of passing off her son as her younger brother may seem absurd. Further on we shall see, however, that there can be no doubt that it is the fact, since Martin Constantine Haryett (after the death of his mother) established his identity first in France and then in England.

The fortune, given Miss Howard by the father of her son, consisted in the main of houses on lease and building lots in London admirably situated for new development. The value of this real estate never ceased to increase throughout the whole of her life. In Nathaniel Strode,[1] she had an excellent trustee who looked after Miss Howard's affairs until her death, and even beyond, making well-considered investments fructify on her behalf. It is uncertain whether she was precisely aware of the importance of her fortune, but she took pleasure in living in a

[1] Nathaniel William John Strode (1816–89), financier and landowner, acquired, among other country houses, Camden Place, Chislehurst, which he decorated " in the French taste " with furniture bought in Paris. The husband of Eleanor Margaret Courtney, Strode died at Bray Court, Maidenhead, on the 26th February, 1889.

grand style. Her elegance was a byword; her horses and carriages created a sensation; a well-drilled staff were in charge of Rockingham House. Never was precocious immorality more sumptuously embowered.

Miss Howard shone in a marginal society, the English version of that painted by Alexandre Dumas the Younger, in " Le Demi-Monde." She was received in a few of the more easy-going houses, those open to artists and even to the ladies of the theatre. Lady Blessington invited her to Gore House.

At over fifty, the Countess of Blessington, the legitimate widow of a peer of the realm, found herself cut off from the Victorian court and from the more exclusive houses. In those days it was a misfortune to create scandal. Margaret Power, a beautiful Irishwoman, was, like Elizabeth Ann Haryett, of plebeian origin. Married young to an alcoholic, Maurice St. Leger Farmer, she had immediately left him to run away with a first lover, with whom she lived on an estate in Hampshire. Her second lover had been Viscount Mountjoy, future Lord Blessington and cousin to Major Mountjoy Martyn. When Farmer was killed in a drunken brawl, Viscount Mountjoy, recently widowed and become Earl of Blessington, married his mistress. The latter immediately took a third lover: Alfred, Count d'Orsay, " Cupidon unchained," the best-looking of Frenchmen and the personification of elegance.

They all three lived happily together. Lord Blessington, not only a complaisant husband but a pervert, wished to enrich the handsome Alfred. He decided to marry off his own daughter, Lady Harriet Gardiner, who was his sole heiress, to his wife's lover. The future wife, then aged twelve, was not consulted. The three accomplices together decided that the marriage would not be consummated. The wedding was solemnised at Naples when the girl was fifteen years old. The latter developed a hatred for her husband and, naturally enough, for Lady Blessington too.

Having thus heaped scandal upon scandal, Lady Blessington

could not expect to be received in the best society. She stayed at home and contented herself with having a salon in London, in Paris and even, for six years, at Genoa, Florence, and Naples.

" Her dinners were served on beautiful plate; the wines flowed in profusion. A cosmopolitan world lent a certain piquancy; without being loose, the tone was more liberal there than elsewhere. Politicians, writers and painters were received graciously by an incomparable hostess . . ." [1]

Major Mountjoy Martyn, cousin by marriage to Lady Blessington, brought Miss Howard to her house where her beauty caused a sensation. In these fresh surroundings, Harriet took on a new personality. Nothing precisely was known of her past life. She was a courtesan, of course, but an English courtesan, immensely secretive and discreet. She was the product of a country where libertinage itself wears a mask of ideal distinction.

At one of the brilliant receptions given at Gore House in the month of June 1846, Alfred d'Orsay wished to introduce Miss Howard to the guest of honour of the evening. He advised her to make her best curtsey to the newcomer, whom he himself addressed as *Monseigneur* and *Son Altesse Imperiale*. She curtseyed exactly as she would have done in some historic drama before Richard II or Henry VIII. The august personage, who spoke in a strong German accent, since he had been educated at Augsburg in Bavaria, deigned to address a few gracious words to her.

Raising her eyes, Harriet saw a man who, for all his shortness of stature, had a commanding presence and expressed himself with a sort of majestic shyness. There was a disproportion between the size of his head and the shortness of his body. Beneath a huge forehead, his eyes seemed veiled in sorrow. But the dignity of his manner commanded respect. A con-

[1] Élisabeth de Gramont, *Le Comte d'Orsay et Lady Blessington*, p. 37.

spirator in exile, having escaped from the prisons to which his judges had condemned him for life, he spoke of them without hatred and of himself without boasting.

He was Prince Louis Napoleon Bonaparte, son of Hortense, Queen of Holland, and grandson of Josephine, Empress of the French.

CHAPTER TWO

HARRIET IN LOVE

UPON THE death of the Duke of Reichstadt, born King of Rome and son of the Eagle, his cousin Louis Napoleon had become, in 1832, head of the Bonaparte family and thus pretender to the Empire.

Brought up in exile, affiliated since adolescence to the *Carbonari*, the tense atmosphere of conspiracy was his natural element. In 1836 he had made a first attempt at a military uprising at Strasbourg. In order to prevent his acquiring a martyr's halo, Louis Philippe, a good-natured king, had merely sent him to the United States of America. Nevertheless, after a second daring attempt upon the beaches of Boulogne in 1840, Louis Napoleon was arrested, arraigned before the Court of Peers and condemned to perpetual imprisonment. When he saw the Fortress of Ham, in which he was to be imprisoned, the Prince asked: " How long does perpetuity last here? " The prisoner proposed, as he said, " to continue his studies at the University of Ham." His imprisonment lasted six years. In his cell he wrote a book, which was praised by George Sand, and fathered two illegitimate children. These were the relaxations of an imprisoned prince!

In all romantic novels about prisons, the heroine is the gaoler's too-kind-hearted daughter. This particular one was called Alexandrine-Éléonore Vergeot[1]; the people of Ham called her

[1] Born 1820, died 1886.

" the Beautiful Clog-dancer." Her father appointed her bed-maker to State Prisoner No. 1. When the latter saw her bringing up his meals, he offered to educate her and proposed, in particular, " lessons in orthography and grammar." He taught her so well that she gave birth to two future Counts of the Second Empire.[1] A humble idyll behind prison bars.

On the 25th May, 1846, Louis Napoleon succeeded in escaping. In order to get out of the fortress, he borrowed the clothes of a mason called Badinguet, and won thereby the nickname his enemies always applied to him when he had become Emperor. After his escape, he took refuge in London, playing the part of a fashionable exile in the drawing-rooms of Belgravia, while secretly preparing his political revenge. Conspiracy was his strong point. Once upon a time, Hortense, at the Tuileries, " had succeeded in being thought frivolous while possessing the capacity of a statesman"; her two surviving sons inherited similar capabilities.

The Prince dined out, sometimes at Lady Malmesbury's, sometimes at the Duchess of Somerset's. He rowed upon the Thames with the Disraeli family. But his heedlessness was only pretence; he was preparing himself to reign.

Since Napoleon I had died, " nailed to a desert rock," and a citizen king had occupied the throne of France in bourgeois state, the English were quite prepared to become Bonapartists. A contemporary print shows the young exile against a romantic landscape; beneath the portrait, which depicts him as both handsome and melancholy, is written, " Prince Louis-Napoleon, the victim of Louis-Philippe."

Received at first from mere curiosity, the refugee was soon sympathetically taken up. Moreover, two near relations assured their cousin solid support among the English aristocracy: Lady

---

[1] At their baptism, they each received the Christian names of their father and mother, followed by a third name: (1) Alexandre-Louis-Eugène, born in 1843, later Comte d'Orx, secretary to the Embassy in St. Petersburg, then French Consul in Zanzibar. He died in January 1910; (2) Alexandre-Louis-Ernest, born 1845, later Comte de Labenne, and an official of the Inland Revenue. He died in 1882.

Dudley Stuart, who was the daughter of Lucien Bonaparte[1]; and the Marchioness of Douglas, whose mother was a Beauharnais.[2]

From diplomatic prudence the Court treated him with reserve, but Louis Napoleon was elected a member of three great clubs: the Athenæum, the Army and Navy, and the Junior United Services. He delighted in asking artists to tea. Among his friends were Thomas Moore, Edwin Landseer, Macready, Thackeray and Dickens. He was considered an interesting personality because, after two setbacks, he still refused to believe that he would not one day reign over France. Indeed, he expounded his liberal programme with the calm assurance of a reformer who is about to achieve power.

The newspapers, which were always kind to him, created for him a certain popularity. When he went out, there was always a number of loungers gathered at his door to catch a glimpse of him. They saluted him politely.

The habits of the landed gentry coincided perfectly with the Prince's tastes. A good horseman himself, he took a great interest in the turf. Having become " the lion of the season," he spent week-ends in country houses; shooting parties were organised in his honour. During a stay at Cam House, which belonged to Mrs. Dawson-Damer, Louis Bonaparte said to Lord Alvanley: " It is written that ere long I shall become Emperor of France, avenge the defeat of Waterloo and drive the Austrians out of Italy."[3] Because he believed himself created by Providence to restore a throne and assure the continuity of a dynasty, he

---

[1] Christine Égypta (1798–1847) was the daughter of Lucien Bonaparte, Prince de Canino, and of his first wife Christine Boyer. Divorced from the Swede, Arved Posse, whom she had married in 1818, she was married again, in 1826, to Lord Dudley Stuart.

[2] Princess Marie of Baden (1817–88), wife of William, Marquess of Douglas, later 11th Duke of Hamilton (1811–63), was the third daughter of the marriage of Stephanie de Beauharnais, the adopted daughter of Napoleon I, to Charles Louis, reigning Grand-Duke of Baden.

[3] Quoted by Shane Leslie in his Introduction to The Letters of Mrs. Fitzherbert, the adoptive mother of Mrs. Dawson-Damer, p. xxvi.

audaciously took precedence over everyone present. The firmness evident in this attitude elicited respect in itself.

To Sir Edward Bulwer, Whig member for Lincoln, he sent a copy of his book entitled, *Des idées napoléoniennes*, which had won the praise of George Sand. Under the author's autographed dedication, Bulwer wrote:

> " The book of a very able mind; with few ideas, but those ideas bold, large and reducible to vigorous action ... Prince Louis Napoleon has qualities that may render him a remarkable man if he ever returns to France. Dogged, daring, yet somewhat reserved and close, he can conceive with secrecy and act with promptitude. His faults would come from conceit and rashness; but akin with these characteristics are will and enthusiasm. He has these in a high degree. Above all, he has that intense faith in his own destiny with which men rarely fail of achieving something great ..." [1]

From which it can be seen that politicians were as taken with him as was the fashionable world.

Women were charmed by him. Lady Holland said, " If he had rather longer legs, he would be Prince Charming!"

Thick-set, too short in the body but looking well in the saddle, Louis Bonaparte was almost imposing on horseback and well knew it. This perhaps was why he had so great a liking for riding. Harriet Howard was, undoubtedly, the woman most likely to please him. Was she not the queen of horsewomen?

Louis Napoleon as an almost poverty-stricken refugee had the double prestige of being both an outlaw and a member of a royal family. That he should have twice risked his life to restore the Empire delighted the romantic tragedy actress, imbued as she was with myth and legend. Everything about him enchanted her: his restricted childhood, his hostile parents, his membership of the Carbonari with their strange rites of initiation, his disastrous conspiracies, his life-sentence and, above all, his miraculous escape. So many episodes in his life seemed positively Shake-

[1] Quoted by Ivor Guest in *Napoleon III in England*, p. 39.

spearean! How could a Drury Lane actress fail to see in this Prince the prototype of her heart's desire?

He was touched by the admiration that his life story, even with its double setback, inspired in so beautiful a woman. When Lady Blessington asked him to recount some of his adventures to her guests, it was Miss Howard whom he addressed, for her alone that he spoke. She was profoundly moved. Without taking his eyes from her, he gave to the narration of his hard apprentice years an epic quality. Harriet, entranced, believed she was listening to an epic poem from the lips of its hero. Achilles reciting *The Iliad*, dedicating it to her alone, could not have affected her more profoundly than did this Bonaparte when, in Lady Blessington's drawing-room, he evoked his uncle and his destiny.

Two strangers had here met for the first time. They had expected nothing from the meeting. But they were struck by an immemorial, a reciprocal flash of lightning. They felt that they were made for each other and that nothing could prevent their union.

They met again during the following days. Miss Howard, humble, penitent, had to confess that she had been living with a married man for the last five years. Her sin was at once forgiven her. (She did not mention the "horse-coper".) When the penitent shyly admitted that she had an illegitimate son, the Prince replied that he had two.

"The fruits of captivity!" he murmured, shrugging his shoulders unconcernedly.

The fact was that he gave no thought to the unimportant Alexandrine Vergeot. Among other advantages, his escape had put an end to a somewhat undignified liaison.

When the exile and the actress became lovers, she murmured, "It was written!" The giving of herself was linked in her mind with some idea of predestination, of a mission to fulfil. Although the Prince always showed his English friends an unshakeable confidence in his star, he was subject, nevertheless, to moods of discouragement.

To Bulwer, he quoted a phrase of Lamartine's: " France is bored! " And said that he felt certain of succeeding Louis-Philippe. To Disraeli he categorically affirmed: " I have received important news from France. Two thousand young officers have stated in writing that they will fight for a Bonaparte restoration! "

Was it in fact true that the French army was whole-heartedly in favour of the Pretender? He had succeeded neither at Strasbourg nor at Boulogne in raising more than a handful of soldiers. It was only to Miss Howard that he admitted a doubt as to his popularity.

Harriet renewed his twice-disappointed hopes. She had faith in him. A British subject, she was nevertheless ready to become an expatriate in order to follow her Bonaparte wherever it might please him to go in search of adventure. A millionairess, she was prepared to offer her whole fortune to the Napoleonic cause. Never was a woman more utterly devoted. Partisan, intoxicated with self-abnegation, she was prepared to sacrifice her casket to the last jewel in order to assure the success of the enterprise. She prayed the eternal conspirator to allow her to share his risks, even if it entailed mortal danger.

In anguished, anxious hours, she often invoked Shakespeare's name. Like a mad sibyl, she often quoted her first tragic role to her lover.

> Be lion-mettled, proud, and take no care
> Who chafes, who frets, or where conspirers are;
> Macbeth shall never vanquish'd be until
> Great Birnam wood to high Dunsinane hill
> Shall come against him.

She put a personal interpretation upon these lines: a Napoleon is invincible. He cannot be defeated unless the trees themselves are changed into enemy soldiers to attack him!

When Miss Howard was inspired to talk thus, she could not foresee to what extent the prophecy from *Macbeth* would later become relevant to her hero. To-day, we know that, as she foretold, Napoleon III achieved his crown. We know, too, that the day would come when the Celtic *Ar Dean*, the army of oaks, would conceal from the eyes of the encircled French the invisible vice in which the German troops held them; and that, at Sedan, in the dark forest of Ardenne, the vanquished Emperor would have to surrender his sword.

In 1846, however, 1870 was unforeseeable and, in the meantime, the English summer was delightful. The unfortunate Prince, " the victim of Louis Philippe," was engaged in a delicious adventure. Miss Howard was madly in love with him.

* * *

Harriet suddenly realised that she was moving from the theatrical world on to the plane of world history. What can a woman, who is really in love, do to make herself worthy of a glorious destiny but endeavour to put some kind of order into her life? Athirst for propriety, Miss Howard pursued a double objective: she wished to see her beloved Napoleon ascend a throne; she wanted the Prince to be the instrument of her redemption.

If it is true that Eros, the son of Aphrodite, demands human sacrifices, Major Mountjoy Martyn was destined to become the expiatory victim, the burnt sacrifice, offered up to the jealous young god. Could the companion of a reigning sovereign remain semi-married to an officer of the British Army?

Miss Howard set about breaking her principal liaison with an impetuous haste that Bonaparte had not required, foreseen, or even desired. Wishing to present the two men with the accomplished fact, she immediately confessed to the major that she had never loved him.

Their union, she said, had been no more than a sensible and convenient arrangement for a poor orphan alone in the world and dishonoured by Mason. Passion had at last been revealed to her. A great prince had fallen in love with her. She was in love with him. Too loyal to betray, even in secret, the father of her son, she had come to him spontaneously to reveal the state of her conscience. Let him decide.

As a perfect gentleman, what was he to do? Was he forcibly to retain a woman who wished to resume her liberty? The major felt unable to do anything of the sort. A chivalrous man, he accepted the rupture without manifesting his chagrin, which was nevertheless lively, since even a gentleman is none the less a man.

Since Martin's birth, Harriet had been an exemplary mother. Nevertheless, it seemed natural to her to separate the child from his father, even at the risk of depriving him of essential support and natural affection. This, alas, is often the case. No woman can be at once a good mother and passionately in love. The choice has to be made, and she chooses the lover.

In order to reconcile the two conflicting emotions of her passionate nature, Miss Howard set about creating a link between " her unhappy Prince " and the major's son. When, much later, Martin was created a Count of the Empire, public opinion saw in his ennoblement a tacit, significant but quite illusory admission of paternity. In support of this legend, it would be said that Louis Napoleon had taken Harriet Howard as mistress, not in 1846, but before Strasbourg and America, that is to say in 1836. The legend implied that the intrepid horsewoman had succeeded in entering the fortress of Ham in November 1841 and had left it pregnant with her only child. Gossip on the margin of history. Those who place the beginning of this famous liaison at 1836 forget that Elizabeth Ann Haryett was only thirteen in that year.

When Prince Bonaparte made his conquest of her, she was a woman of twenty-three. She had become much more sophisticated since the day when, blushing and ashamed, she had pretended to be the elder sister of her child. At Rockingham House, Martin was king. His mother showed him off with pride.

It is easy to understand how Louis Napoleon, a homeless refugee and in love with Miss Howard, might easily, under the sway of mutual passion, become attached to the attractive child. It was at this time that he offered his mistress the guardianship of the children of Alexandrine Vergeot. These "fruits of imprisonment" were discreetly brought up at Batignolles-Monceaux by the Prince's own nurse, Colette Bure. Later, when he had become Emperor, he was in fact to confide the august bastards to Miss Howard's care. They were of approximately the same age as Martin.[1] When, towards the end of his reign Napoleon III poured lands, blazons and titles upon his favourites, the three boys were all ennobled by the titles of their estates. It was a perfectly natural thing to do.

In the light of what followed, historians have been unable to see Miss Howard as other than an intriguer, greedy for honours and wealth. They have maintained that Harriet, great race-goer as she was, betting on her lover as she might have punted on a horse, backed Bonaparte to win. But this is to forget their respective positions in 1846. Miss Howard, a fashionable beauty, lived opulently in London with the father of her child. "At her table," wrote Comte Fleury, "were to be found the most distinguished men of the aristocracy . . . the Duke of Beaufort, Lord Chesterfield, Lord Malmesbury and a dozen other fashionable men were intimate members of her circle . . ."[2] When the Prince Pretender made his first appearance, he was loaded with debts and had recently been six years in prison. The chances of a Napoleonic restoration, after two notorious setbacks, seemed small. Nevertheless Harriet, falling in love with the refugee, never hesitated to sacrifice to him the rich man by whom she had had a son. It was of her own volition that she left Rockingham House, where all was "order and beauty, luxury, peace" and security. With the agreement of her trustees, she took a small but charming house, No. 9 Berkeley Street. She at once

---

[1] Martin was born in 1842, Eugène in 1843 and Louis in 1845.
[2] *Souvenirs du général comte Fleury*, Vol. I, p. 205.

offered the Prince, who was very short of money, board and lodging. They spent two years of happiness together there.

Miss Howard, who was the victim of many libels (invented during the Second Empire by the political adversaries of the régime) accusing her of the licentious morals of a street-walker, open to suggestions from the first comer, was in fact so little shameless that she always preferred living with a single lover to independence. A dissolute woman would have preferred freedom; Harriet, living in concubinage, always presented the most respectable exterior. Her house was well ordered; her manners were irreproachable; she would never have permitted lewd or indecent conversation at her table. During the course of three successive liaisons, she lived as a wife in circumstances of at least semi-conjugality.

The years 1846 to 1848 were years of waiting and expectation. Louis Napoleon was preparing himself for the exercise of power; Miss Howard for the delicate role of Imperial Egeria. To remedy the obvious lacunae in her education, she spent all her mornings in study with eminent teachers. Her history master was Alexander William Kinglake,[1] who had just published a classic book of travel in the Orient: *Eothen*. This brilliant, cynical writer, the friend of Tennyson and Thackeray, had remained a bachelor because, so he said, " Women always prefer other men to their husbands."

Kinglake found it impossible to instruct Miss Howard in history without falling in love with her. From the very first lessons, the master wished to make a mistress of his indignant pupil. Harriet defended herself. She looked upon the impudent familiarities of the audacious man of learning as outrages upon decency. He saw in her an infuriated Lucretia.

The master was disillusioned. Miss Howard was looked upon as a light woman and an easy conquest. Had she not had rich

---

[1] Alexander William Kinglake (1809–91), historian and politician. He followed the campaign in the Crimea and was present at the Battle of the Alma. Elected for Bridgwater, he was Member of Parliament from 1857–68.

protectors before this idyll with her Prince? Was she legally married to Prince Bonaparte? Harriet was to learn to her cost that a woman, who has twice sold herself, and who is allied to a third lover, can no longer refuse her favours to a fourth without making of him an implacable enemy. " After I had made my first decisions," George Sand said, " I no longer had the right to demand mere friendship. Men only give their love in friendship regretfully. They expect to indulge their senses through the tender affections they experience."

Historians can bide their time. Kinglake was to wait fifteen years for the opportunity of avenging his humiliation upon his happy rival. When Lord Raglan commissioned him to write the *History of the Crimean War*, Kinglake drew a ferocious portrait of Napoleon III in his eight volume *magnum opus*.

Comte Fleury, who was witness in London to Harriet's passion for the Prince, his intimate friend, cannot be suspected of any particular goodwill towards her whom, in his *Souvenirs*, he always calls " the Courtesan." Nevertheless, the austere Fleury admits that Miss Howard had " incomparable beauty "; and adds farther on:

" Whether from devotion or ambition, this charming English-woman definitely told her lover that she desired nothing but to serve him and that, for him, she would give up all her luxury, success and social triumphs . . . It is impossible to deny that this lacked neither generosity nor disinterestedness . . ." [1]

Thus Miss Howard shared her Berkeley Street house with the Prince. He called her " my landlady " or " my fair hostess." Their living together shocked not only the more strait-laced English, but also the French living in London. These latter were numerous at this time for, whenever there is a revolution in Paris, refugees cross the channel.

For example in 1848 Gabriel Delessert, Prefect of Police in the July monarchy, fearing arrest after the events of February,

[1] *Souvenirs du général comte Fleury*, Vol. I, p. 206.

had crossed over to England. His whole family had followed him. Alexis de Valon, the young husband of Cécile Delessert and a fervent Orléaniste, noted with some displeasure the growing popularity of Louis Napoleon. We find him writing to his mother in a mocking, ironical tone about the Prince Pretender and the actress without parts.

June 24th 1848.—I have the frequent happiness of meeting Prince Louis here, one of those names one invokes in the general penury of the times, one of those straws one clutches at when upon the point of drowning . . . It is sufficient to see the little man, common and ill-famed as he is, to realise the vanity of the hopes placed in him! He doesn't match up to the part they want him to play. Imagine a little man, four and a half feet high, ugly and vulgar, with huge moustaches and pigs' eyes. So much for his outward appearance. From the moral point of view, he lives publicly, to the great scandal of English propriety, with a tenth rate actress, who is however extremely beautiful, called Miss Howard. This behaviour, which has gradually closed every door to him in London high society, throws him back upon the society of actors . . .[1]

On the 23rd February, 1848, Louis Philippe I, King of the French by the Grace of God and the Tricolour, had been dethroned.

" I believe—" said Louis Napoleon—" I believe that, from time to time, men are born whom I would call *providential*, into whose hands the destinies of their countries are confided. I believe that I am one of those men."

France was to take him at his word.

[1] Letter from Alexis de Valon (1818–51) to his mother, Comtesse Joseph de Valon, née Anne de Gaudechart. Maurice Parturier quotes it in a note to his edition of the *Correspondance générale de Prosper Mérimée*, Vol. V, p. 332.

CHAPTER THREE

THE PRINCE-PRESIDENT

IF ONE is to believe Lamartine, the February days which were fatal to the July Monarchy " surprised the world." The floodtide of revolution having washed Louis Philippe on to the English shore, the ebb deposited Louis Napoleon upon the French coast of the Channel. In Paris the political situation was confused. The Republic, the second of that name, had been proclaimed. A provisional government of eleven members, a strange nest of vipers, exercised power. The country was unstable and disunited.

The Royalist Party was divided into two opposed factions, of which each had its own Pretender. The Orléanists wished to bring back to the Tuileries Louis Philippe II (the Comte de Paris, in whose favour his grandfather had abdicated); the Legitimists remained faithful to Henry V, the last of the elder branch, who, born Duc de Bordeaux, bore in exile the title of Comte de Chambord. Similarly, the Republican Party was divided into a number of hostile groups. Lamartine, the romantic poet, represented the moderate tendency; Ledru-Rollin, a moustachioed Hercules, preached a Socialist doctrine, and little Louis Blanc waved the red flag of a proletarian demagogue. These divisions and subdivisions were to be an advantage to the renaissance of Bonapartism.

France, covered with glory by Napoleon I, opened wide her arms to the heirs of that sublime name. Three of the Emperor's nephews (Pierre Bonaparte, son of Lucien; Napoleon, son of ex-King Jérôme of Westphalia; and Lucien Murat, son of Caroline, ex-Queen of Naples) were, in April 1848, elected members of the Constituent Assembly. Louis Napoleon Bonaparte, head of the family, had not wished his candidature to be put forward. But, in a similar election in June, four departments chose him as their representative. This time he went. With the innate tact of Englishwomen, Miss Howard did not accompany him; she joined him later. The Prince, having established his headquarters in the Place Vendôme, at the Hôtel du Rhin, she went to the Meurice which was, even in those days, the favourite hotel of the English gentry. Unknown in Paris, she limited herself to leading a simple and retired life.

Lamartine anxiously tried to prove that the support for Napoleon lacked substance. " There are," he said, " moments of aberration among the masses; there are names which attract the multitude like a red rag does a bull! . . ." But Jules Favre took up the Prince's defence, and Louis Blanc himself cried: " Let the Emperor's nephew draw near to the sun of our Republic; he will be annihilated by its heat! . . ."

Quiet, taciturn, silent, the Prince took his place on the left-wing benches and Victor Hugo, future author of *Châtiments*, wrote: " He is not a Prince; but an idea. The people have not elected the blunderer of Boulogne, but the victor of Iéna! . . . His candidature dates from Austerlitz."

The " honourable member Louis Bonaparte " was a bad speaker. He mumbled at the tribune and showed himself incapable of improvisation. His incompetence reassured those whom his presence had disconcerted. " He's unintelligent," said M. Thiers. " He's a fool whom we shall be able to lead." And Ledru-Rollin said triumphantly, " What an idiot! He's finished."

When the Prince interviewed his political agents, Miss Howard was at his side, but without ostentatious familiarity. Always beautifully dressed, content to belong to the decorative species of "fair listeners," she never even asked a question. Political discussions frequently took place in the presence of this silent foreigner. She never took part in them. People watched her, looked upon her as an enigma. She expressed herself merely by smiles of approbation, an expression of intelligence, gestures of approval. Her extreme reserve was lauded. Her silence was her strength, since she knew very little French.

The two lovers went for long rides on horseback in the Forest of Saint-Germain and the woods of Meudon. It was not long before this was remarked upon. A clubman was heard to say, "Who said that Prince Louis Napoleon lacked intelligence? He has brought from London the most beautiful woman and the most beautiful horse in the world!" The thoroughbred mare was called Lizzie. The favourite was "a beautiful woman about whom one might easily be mistaken," and since her surname of Howard was that of the Dukes of Norfolk, the Prince's mysterious companion was at first taken for an Englishwoman of quality. It was then learnt that the electoral campaign of the candidate for the Presidency of the Republic was largely financed by this radiant figure from the Society Journals.

On the 10th December, 1848, 5,434,226 voters, out of 7,327,345 votes recorded, elected His Imperial Highness Prince Louis Napoleon Bonaparte to the first Magistracy of the Second Republic. It was a triumph. He moved into the Élysée, his official residence. Miss Howard took a small house at 14 Rue du Cirque, whose back-door gave on to the Avenue Marigny. To go from the Presidential garden to that of his beloved, the Prince had only to cross the quiet, deserted street.

For Harriet 1849 was the *annus mirabilis*. The Prince-President was in power and loved her more devotedly than ever. The intimates of the Élysée, overawed by her great beauty, treated her as the master's "official mistress." Even the prude Fleury became more tractable. We find in the first volume of his *Souvenirs*:

" The Marquess of Hertford,[1] Persigny, Ney, Toulongeon, Béville sometimes went to dine or pass the evening with her, in company with the Prince. We found there certain hangers-on whom she had gathered round her because of her fortune . . . Moreover, Mocquard and Comte Bacciochi had become her intimates. A few foreigners, a doctor, and a number of artists were part of this intimate society. Together they formed a discreet little court . . . It goes without saying that there were few women. This is always the case with irregular liaisons. There were one or two 'lady companions' who made up the female society . . . As long as Louis-Napoleon remained the soldier in the breach, rather than the definitive head of the government, this little-advertised liaison, which was unknown to the great mass of the public, led to very little inconvenience. Their life was organised with propriety and complete discretion . . . The Prince was a bachelor; and practically none of us was married. Nothing, therefore, in this behaviour could offend public opinion . . ."[2]

The fourth Marquess of Hertford, of whom Fleury speaks, was the most Parisian of all Englishmen. The owner of Bagatelle, in the Bois de Boulogne, he also possessed the superb town house of Brancas-Lauraguais in the Rue Cerutti, and another house at the angle of the Boulevard des Italiens and the Rue Taitbout. He so loved Paris that he spent the last fourteen years of his life there, without ever returning to his native country and chose, for his grave, the cemetery of Père-Lachaise. We shall see that he was the faithful friend of Miss Howard, and remained so till his death.

When he came to the Rue du Cirque, he often brought with him his brother, Lord Henry Seymour, another francophile, whom the witty populace called " Milord l'Arsouille—my lord Cad "; Paris owes to him the foundation of both the Société d'Encouragement and the Jockey Club.

A young man of some thirty years of age always accompanied

[1] Richard Seymour Conway, Viscount Beauchamp, later Earl of Yarmouth, and finally fourth Marquess of Hertford (1800–70), was the eldest son of Francis Charles Seymour Conway, third Marquess of Hertford, and of Maria Emily Fagnani.
[2] *Souvenirs du général comte Fleury*, Vol. I.

the two noble lords, to whom he was known to be related. Their mother, widow of the third Marquess of Hertford, had brought this young man up and always introduced him as " Richard Wallace, my dear nephew." In fact, he was her grandson. To him, Paris owes a hundred public fountains and London a magnificent museum.

He had been born in London,[1] the illegitimate son of an eighteen-year-old undergraduate, who was heir presumptive to the marquisate of Hertford (and the future friend of Harriet Howard). At his baptism Richard had been given his father's Christian name; much later, his mother's name became legally his. Born Agnes Wallace,[2] this woman of good family but deplorable morals had ultimately abandoned what can only be called an episodic husband in order to lead a dissolute life under the pseudonym of Mrs. Jackson. Twelve years older than her lover, wild Agnes went to Brighton where she became the public property of the 10th Hussars which was in garrison there and had for Colonel the Prince of Wales. When the child was born, she evaded the duties of maternity as she had earlier evaded those of marriage. Luckily, Lady Hertford, whose son could clearly not bring up an infant at the University of Oxford, took charge of Richard. He grew up in his indulgent grandmother's house and was never to leave her again.

Like history, family scandals often repeat themselves. Lord Hertford had begotten this only and unrecognised son by an adolescent affair. When barely of age, Richard Wallace had also to face the consequences of premature and illicit parenthood. The Parisian woman, who had been his mistress since 1839, was without beauty or culture, for which she atoned by an indomitable obstinacy.

Julie Castelnau worked as a saleswomen in a scent shop, which the dandies had made fashionable, in the Passage du

---

[1] On the 2nd June, 1818.
[2] Agnes Wallace (1789–1864) was the daughter of Sir Thomas Wallace of Craigie. She had married Samuel Bickley on the 12th August, 1808.

The Château de Beauregard about 1873

The Château de Beauregard in 1956

The Emperor Napoleon III by Hippolyte Flandrin

Saumon. One day, a new customer appeared at the counter. The cunning girl immediately set her cap at this well-dressed, attractive and reserved young Englishman, who expressed himself with such ceremonious politeness. The conquest of Richard Wallace proved rapid and easy because of his extreme shyness.

A bastard, baptised Edmond-Richard, was born on the 27th August, 1840, " at his mother's, Julie-Amélie-Charlotte Castelnau, 10 Rue Blanche." Kindly Wallace would undoubtedly have been perfectly prepared to marry his mistress, but Lord Hertford, a declared enemy of the institution of marriage, held despotic sway over his family. He would never have permitted such a union and the question did not arise.

At about this time Julie got herself introduced to Miss Howard. In a house denuded of women, the first come is warmly welcomed. But everyone present wondered how such a perfect gentleman as Wallace could have attached himself to such a second-rate woman. Compared to Miss Howard, who was discreet and lady-like, Mademoiselle Castelnau made a very bad impression. Always sulky and surly, eternally discontented, she was not popular in this circle. They let her grumble and paid her no further attention.

Fleury also mentions among the frequenters of Miss Howard's salon, Jean Mocquard,[1] whom Queen Hortense, in her last days, had held in great esteem. " A man of wit, a great conversationalist and delightfully well-read, Mocquard had a family inheritance of intellect: through his mother, he was descended from the celebrated Bussy-Rabutin. He himself had a gift of style and knew Bossuet better than anyone else ... He had long been a friend of Prince Louis and his devotion dated back many years ..."[2] It was in memory of his dead mother that the Prince-President had formed a friendship with this man so worthy of his confidence.

[1] Jean-François-Constant Mocquard (1791–1864). He was successively *sous-préfet*, private secretary, then *Chef de Cabinet* to Napoleon III, and a senator.
[2] *Souvenirs du général comte Fleury*, Vol. I, p. 64.

Dr. Ménière wrote in his *Journal*:

> For intimate secretary, or perhaps one should say for intimate friend, he has M. Mocquard who has now been with him for a long time. I like Mocquard very much. Fairly tall, very thin, his features have a certain severity of aspect, but underlying his appearance is much wit, gaiety, intelligence and friendliness . . . He has a passion for old books. He owns a huge folio Tacitus with great margins in which he makes notes. He spends his time trying to find analogies between the men of our time and those the great historians so forcefully depict . . .[1]

Jean Mocquard was to become *chef de cabinet* to the Prince-President (and until his death, was to remain in that post, to Emperor Napoleon III). Closely associated with the preparation of the *coup d'état*, he was of all the sovereign's intimates the least inclined to indiscretions. The Emperor made Amédée Mocquard, a lawyer from Provins and son of his friend, successor to Maître Noël who, having been lawyer to Napoleon I, had then become his own.

Miss Howard's happiness lacked but one thing: the joys of respectability. She cleverly made overtures to the British Embassy. Since she was a British citizen, it was natural that she should make contact with the Envoy Extraordinary and Plenipotentiary of Her Majesty. Lord Normanby, a witness to the remarkable success of his beautiful compatriot, thought it sensible to support her dawning pre-eminence. To consolidate Miss Howard's position, he presented her to Lady Normanby and invited her to the Embassy receptions. The more prudish French were shocked: " Lord Normanby, a diplomat of the eighteenth-century school, had established himself in the good graces of Louis Napoleon by meeting, and even by making his wife receive, Miss Howard, the former's mistress," wrote the virtuous Alexis de Tocqueville.[2] Count de Bark, a Swedish

---

[1] *Journal du docteur Prosper Ménière*, edited by his son, p. 441.
[2] *Souvenirs d'Alexis de Tocqueville*, p. 237.

diplomat who, in London, had been a friend of the Prince's (long before his success) followed Lord Normanby's example. He saw no objection to his wife dining with him at Miss Howard's and the latter was well received at the Swedish Legation.

Mocquard, promoted *chef de cabinet*, also did his best to appease Harriet's urgent thirst for respectability. He allowed her to make friends with his wife and daughter, who was not yet married, both of whose reputations were irreproachable. This was very well received. But Harriet, quite insatiable, desired yet more.

On a higher level, she was not received by the Princesse Mathilde, first cousin to the President and " first lady " of the new régime. Not that the latter was particularly strait-laced, she merely conformed to the unwritten laws of her period and her caste. Before taking the good-looking Nieuwerkerque for lover, she had married, at twenty years old, the fabulously wealthy Demidoff, and then had freed herself of him with both scandal and profit. The man she had repudiated paid her alimony on condition that she should never have children, and this clause in the contract of their separation had never been violated. By contrast, the imprudent Harriet, before she had known either love or ambition, had brought discredit upon herself by bringing a bastard into the world.

A witty woman, Princesse Mathilde said amusingly, "Had my uncle not been Emperor, I should probably be selling oranges on the quay at Ajaccio! " Another Emperor uncle, Czar Nicholas I, had agreed to her separation from Anatole Demidoff. At that time in France divorce, which had been abolished under the Restoration, had not yet been re-established. A fashionable woman without a husband had only the right to live in a sort of compensatory concubinage. Such was, in 1849, Mathilde Bonaparte's case. Living publicly with Nieuwerkerque, she imposed her lover upon society, but disliked seeing her cousin the slave of a " hereditary enemy " and dragging " his English chain."

Harriet was never received by Mathilde, who pretended to be ignorant of her existence. To those who wished to present the foreigner to her, she replied with an imperious and imperial refusal, insisting upon the fact that this fallen woman, who had lost her reputation, and had been an unmarried mother for seven years, " was not even married."

The ladies of the Faubourg Saint-Germain followed Princesse Mathilde's example, though their husbands looked upon the outcast with increasing goodwill. When she appeared at his side at a great review, under the command of General Changarnier, the troops were heard to cry: " Long live Napoleon! "

The Maréchal de Castellane wrote in his *Journal* on the 21st May, 1849:

> Mme. Howard, the mistress of the President of the Republic, attended the review in a box; her beauty is most remarkable. Her carriage was very smart; upon the door there is a horse in place of a crest . . .[1]

Significant heraldry. For had not the admiration of a good horseman for a superb horsewoman been the basis of their mutual passion?

[1] *Journal du maréchal de Castellane*, Vol. IV, p. 161.

CHAPTER FOUR

A ROYAL MISTRESS

IN ORDER to maintain his popularity, Louis Napoleon went in person to every town where there was a railway line to inaugurate, a new hospital to visit, an exhibition in need of his patronage or colours to present.

On these occasions, the Prince-President stayed at the Préfecture, his large and numerous suite at an hotel or with local inhabitants. Thus it was that, during an official journey, the house of a certain M. André, receiver-general of finances at Tours, was requisitioned, "for Count Bacciochi,[1] and two ladies." The more beautiful of the two made such a sensation that she lost her incognito. M. André was a Protestant of the most austere morality. When he learnt that the " unmarriable " companion of the head of the State had invited herself to stay in his house in his absence, he was overcome with indignation. From the Pyrenees, where he was taking a cure, the angry civil servant wrote a letter of protest to the President of the Council: " Have we returned to that epoch," he wrote, " when the King's mistresses proclaimed the scandal of their lives throughout the cities of France? . . ."

The President of the Council, in 1849, was that Odilon Barrot, " always dressed in black, neat and tightly buttoned," of whom

---

[1] Comte Félix Bacciochi (1820–66), introducer of ambassadors to the presence, later Superintendent of the Imperial Theatres and Senator, was related to the Bonapartes. His uncle, Félix-Pascal Bacciochi, Prince de Lucques et de Piombino, (1762–1841), had married Élisa Bonaparte, sister of Napoleon I.

Victor Hugo, in *Choses vues*, gives a satirical portrait. Barrot shared the puritanical persuasions of his correspondent. Pleased at being able to give the first Magistrate of the Republic a lesson in propriety, he charged another Barrot (Ferdinand), Secretary-General of the Presidency and his brother, to communicate the virtuous André's letter to the Prince.

President Bonaparte replied with an interminable and ingenuous defence, which is vibrant with his attachment to Miss Howard:

22nd August, 1849.—Your brother has shown me a letter from a certain M. André, to which I should have disdained to reply if it were not full of falsities of fact which ought to be refuted. A lady in whom I am extremely interested, accompanied by a friend of hers and two members of my household, wished to see the horse-show at Saumur. From there she came on to Tours but, fearing not to be able to find a lodging there, she asked me to engage one for her. When I arrived at Tours, I told one of the Councillors in the Préfecture that I wished to find a flat for Comte Bacciochi and for some women friends of his. Chance and their unlucky star led them to M. André where, I do not know why, it was taken for granted that one of them was called Bacciochi. She has never gone by that name. If such an error were committed, it was independently both of my wishes and of those of the lady in question.

Now I should like to know why M. André wishes to make me responsible both for the use of his house and for the false name that was attributed to one person? Does the householder, who makes it his first duty to scrutinise the past lives of those he takes in only in order to decry them, make noble use of hospitality? . . . How many women, a hundred times less pure, a hundred times less devoted, a hundred times less excusable than the one who lodged at M. André's, would have been received with every possible honour by M. André himself, because they would have had the name of their husband to cover their illicit liaisons? I loath this pedantic severity, which ill-disguises a withered heart, is indulgent towards oneself but inexorable where others are concerned. True religion is not intolerant . . .

M. André, whom I am told is a puritan, has not sufficiently

considered the passage in the Evangelist in which Jesus Christ, speaking to people of no greater charity than M. André's, said of a woman whom they wished to stone: " Let him among you, etc." As for myself, I make accusations against no one and I admit myself culpable of seeking, in an illegitimate liaison, the love my heart needs . . .

Since, up to the present, my position has prevented my marrying; since, surrounded with the cares of government, I have in my country, alas, no intimate friends, no childhood acquaintances, no relations who can give me the sweetness of family life, I may well, I believe, be pardoned an affection which does no one any harm and which I make no attempt to proclaim.

To return to M. André, if he believes, as he says, that his house is *polluted* by the presence of a woman who is not married, I pray you to let him know that, for my part, I regret intensely that a person capable of such pure devotion, and of so high a character, should have by chance fallen upon a house where, under the mask of religion, reigns only the ostentation of a pharisaical virtue without Christian charity . . .[1]

The incident created considerable stir. The Prince's advisers took advantage of it to warn him of the dangers of an open liaison. " As loyal friends," wrote Fleury, " our duty was to combat an influence which seemed to us dangerous . . ."[2] Nevertheless, Harriet acquired a new privilege. Her lover having taken possession of the Château of Saint-Cloud, she obtained permission " modestly to hide there," that is to say to occupy the ground-floor apartments which, in a future then unforeseeable, were to become those of the little Prince Imperial.

It is also to be remarked that, two months after " the scandal of Tours," Louis Napoleon wrote to Odilon Barrot to demand his resignation and that of the whole government.

Maréchal de Castellane's Journal, 1849: The President went to luncheon yesterday at Maisons, Madame la Maréchale Ney's

---

[1] *Mémoires posthumes d'Odilon Barrot*, Vol. III, p. 362-3.
[2] *Souvenirs du général comte Fleury*, Vol. I, p. 204.

residence, where the Prince de la Moskowa was in attendance; then he went to Saint-Germain to review the 11th Battalion of the National Guard and the 1st Regiment of Cuirassiers. He presented decorations, then went to the local races. Madame Howard had gone to Saint-Germain with the Prince's *chef de cabinet*, Mocquard, and his wife . . .[1]

Dr. Thomas W. Evans, an American dentist established in Paris, kept an intimate *Journal* as did the Maréchal Comte de Castellane, Émile Fleury, Alexis de Tocqueville, Prosper Ménière, Horace de Viel-Castel and others. Like them, he was much concerned with Miss Howard but abstained out of propriety from mentioning her by name:

During the Prince's residence at the Élysée, I was invited several times to take tea in the evening with him and a few of his intimate friends in a house in the Rue du Cirque . . . This house, where Mme H. lived, was easy of access for him owing to a door in the garden wall of the Palace. The Prince President spent his evenings there, free of constraint, taking a cup of tea or sipping a cup of coffee, smoking a cigarette, with his black dog lying at his feet or upon his knees . . .

He liked listening to music, though he knew little about it, as he himself admitted. What he looked for in this house were the amenities of home life and the conversation of a few intimate friends. Mme Henriette [2]—so she was familiarly called—had only one relation living with her, a young woman of great beauty who was her sister. The grace and simplicity of this young woman fully equalled the beauty of her elder and, one might have said, of her what Mme de Sévigné said of Mlle de Grignan: that she was "a choice and distinguished creature." I used to meet there MM. Fleury, de Persigny, Mocquard, Edgar Ney and a few others only, for there were but very few people of the Prince's circle who were invited to these parties.

The Prince's relations with the beautiful and devoted Mme H. have been censured and have even created a certain scandal. He himself recognised the irregularity of his life, but he was too kind to break with her without some overwhelming motive . . .

[1] *Journal du maréchal de Castellane*, Vol. IV, p. 194.
[2] Henriette is the equivalent in French of the English Christian name, Harriet.

The first time that I went to the house, it was to attend to Mme H. The Prince had said to me that *he would be obliged to me if I would go to her because, if she were seen to come to me, it might give rise to ill-natured gossip.*

Later, as I continued attending Mme H., I sometimes went to visit her in the evening, as I have recounted above . . .[1]

Dr. Evans speaks here of a sister of " Mme Henriette." We know that she never possessed one. The young Englishwoman, whose presence aroused admiration in the American, was called Melliora Findon. She had come from London to fill the position in the Howard household of " reading-woman." The Prince insisted that his mistress should have " lady companions," because he wished to restore her good reputation. We have already seen above how far his anxious solicitude could go: did he not fear that Miss Howard would be criticised, or even compromised, if she were seen going to his dentist?

There was no question of her being able to drive out alone in her carriage in Paris, and less still of her being able to go on foot. It was therefore necessary that she should have a companion, later there were two of them.

Why did she decide to pass off Melliora Findon as her sister? It is an odd point which Harriet never explained. Having learnt to " make up for the injustices of fate," perhaps she wished to invent an imaginary family which she could put in the place of the real one of whom her first fault had deprived her.

It was natural that Miss Howard should wish to marry. She, who had been called " courtesan " at Tours, felt the need of family life and wished to found one. She had a strong maternal instinct. She used to take to the Cirque d'Été not only her own little Martin, as handsome as a Gainsborough page, but also Alexandrine Vergeot's sons, who both bore a remarkable re-

---

[1] *Mémoires du docteur Thomas W. Evans*, p. 3–4.

semblance to their father. The frequent public appearances of the group having been noticed and remarked upon, a certain confusion resulted which was soon to be believed in Parisian drawing-rooms. The grave Odilon Barrot analyses in his *Mémoires* the part Harriet Howard played in Louis Napoleon's life, then states categorically: " This woman had attached herself to him and had even had several children by him." Harriet approved this rumour and took care never to contradict it.

She was certainly encouraged in her ambitions by the British Ambassador; he would have been delighted to see the union between his fellow countrywoman and " the saviour of France " regularised. Supported by Lord Normanby, treated with the utmost respect by her lover's political collaborators, Harriet, like Perrette in the fable, already saw herself Princess-President.

She reasoned about her position, as she did about every other subject, like a patriotic Englishwoman. The Bonapartes, so she thought, being neither Tudors nor Stuarts, the least important Englishwoman was worth the lot of them, Corsican parvenus as they were. To sustain her illusions, she searched the history books for famous examples of outstanding misalliances. The Roi-Soleil had married the widow Scarron, the governess of his illegitimate children, as Miss Howard was governess of the unknown little Bonapartes ... Bianca, née Capello, had died Grand Duchess of Tuscany, and Theodora, whose origins were of the lowest, had become Empress of Constantinople ... A serving-woman, beloved of Peter the Great, had married the Czar and had even succeeded him as reigning sovereign under the name of Catherine I ... All these were admirable precedents.

But, indeed, was Louis Napoleon himself a *true* Bonaparte? All his near relations (except Mathilde) denied it and, among themselves, called him: *Monsieur Beauharnais.* He had been born at a time when the King and Queen of Holland, though not yet officially separated, lived in separate palaces. During the summer of 1807, Louis Bonaparte had received from his all-powerful brother the order to go at once to Toulouse and meet his wife there in order to legalise by his presence the forthcoming birth of their third child. Four years later, in 1811, Queen Hortense, pregnant by the Comte de Flahaut, and finally separated from King Louis, had had to give birth to her fourth son in secret and have the little boy brought up by his maternal grandmother.

From his half-brother the Prince-President was the recipient of valuable political support. Later on, he was to make him first Comte and later Duc de Morny and President of the Legislative Corps. A cousin, Alexandre Walewski (the offspring of a double adultery between Napoleon I and the Comtesse Walewska), was to become his minister for Foreign Affairs. In brief, all these branches of the genealogical tree were loaded with bastards. In such a family Harriet could not believe that the existence of Martin would be held against her in order to do her harm. The man whom she sought to marry had not only an illegitimate brother by his mother, Morny, but one by his father, Castelvecchio, born in Rome in 1806 of an Italian liaison of King Louis.[1]

In 1850 Mme Howard had herself painted lifesize in a gown of English lace over a foundation of rose-coloured satin, a fan in her hand, and two rows of pearls about her neck. This portrait, dated and signed, H. Cappelaere, belongs to-day to her great-grandson, Commandant de la Poix de Fréminville.[2]

During the summer the President visited the Eastern provinces. Harriet accompanied him on the journey. In a letter received by Lord Eddisbury from his wife, dated 31st August, 1850, is a description of the entry into Strasbourg: "Louis Napoleon

---

[1] Francesco Luigi di Castelvecchio to whom Napoleon III gave, in 1860, the title of Comte, died on the 29th May, 1869, at Rennes, as Paymaster-General of Ille-et-Vilaine.

[2] The portrait, here reproduced, is the work of a Parisian woman artist, the pupil of Léon Cogniet. The name of Mlle Henriette Cappelaere is to be found in the catalogue of the *Salons de Peinture* in 1846, 1849, 1851 and 1859. The *Portrait de Madame H—*, hung in the Salon of 1851, is very likely that which the artist painted the year before. She later wrote on the back of the canvas as irrefutable authentication: *Elizabeth Trelawny, Comtesse de Beauregard*.

looked overworked and exhausted . . . Immediately behind the troops came a smart carriage, driven by a woman dressed in the costume of an Alsacian peasant. This woman was Mrs. Howard! . . ."

The following year, she complained for the first time in her life of ill-health; her condition grew quickly worse. The symptoms, as they are described, seem to have been those of an attack of appendicitis, but the operation, which in the twentieth century has become a surgical commonplace, was never then practised. Acute peritonitis placed the patient in grave danger, her lover in agony, and filled Paris with rumours:

" The President of the Republic is very sad," wrote Guizot, the historian, to a friend in the country. " Mme Howard is dying . . . You know who Mme Howard is? A good woman, say those who know her. A beautiful woman, say those who have seen her. I have done neither. She has three children by the President. It is said that she wanted to marry him. He has not married her, but he loves her more than many others, though he loves many others too. He spends his evenings with her, weeping so it is said, while she is in pain. Taken all in all, the President seems to me to be a good enough sort of man . . ." [1]

" She has three children by the President . . ." Like Tocqueville and Odilon Barrot, Guizot vouched for Harriet's fecundity. The fact was that Martin and the children of Alexandrine Vergeot passed all three for having been born in England of the liaison of the Prince with the actress. Miss Howard's attitude towards them gave support to this impression, for she showed an equal tenderness towards them all, calling them " my beloved boys." We shall see later on how, after ten years, Louis and Eugène were torn from her.

Martin, brought up in the certainty that he was the Emperor's

[1] André Gayot, *François Guizot et Madame Laure de Gasparin*, p. 358. The friend to whom this letter was written was Laure de Daunant (1790–1864) who had married, in 1813, Auguste de Gasparin. An incomparable correspondent, Guizot wrote to her regularly for thirty-four years.

son, believed it in all good faith for the rest of his life. And Miss Howard's grandchildren were persuaded of it in turn. It became a family tradition which, transmitted from generation to generation, naturally acquired the strength of conviction.

Two great-grandchildren, still living, have kindly authorised me to reproduce the handsome portrait of their great-grandmother, and to report all the facts I have learned during the course of my researches. I thank them for their kindness and admire their dignified generosity.

*   *   *

Both 1850 and 1851 were years of feverish political intrigue. The President of the Second Republic, elected for four years, was ineligible for re-election; he wished nevertheless to remain at the Élysée. His entertainment allowance of 2,560,000 gold francs seemed to him derisory, for he had a taste for ostentation and lived a life of great pomp and ceremony. From a Parliament composed of legitimists, Orléanists and Republicans, as much as of Bonapartists, the Prince demanded a prolongation of his powers and a supplementary stipend of 1,800,000 francs a year. Thiers, outraged, grumbled: "Not a single penny, not a single day!"

The problem of the future being thus brought to the fore, the legal solution would have been a revision of the constitution. The Assembly, having little inclination to commit suicide, was opposed to it. Powerless and divided as it was, the Chamber nevertheless displayed a common desire to obstruct every measure which might increase the power of an individual. To the Prince-President they refused both prorogation and endowment. Louis Napoleon resolved therefore to " make an Eighteenth Brumaire " and to impose his will by force.

The subtle and cynical Morny, the illegitimate grandson of Talleyrand, was the most suitable man to organise a *coup d'état*. A small but resolute group had formed round Prince Napoleon, and Morny took command of it. They were intent upon defying the Assembly and their object was to make the Presidency life-long.

To put their plans into operation, they had to shackle the army, maintain secret agents wherever public opinion was created, in drawing-rooms, cafés, clubs, and newspaper offices, finance police sports, and send spies into the provinces. The cost of conspiracy would be high.

A few financier friends of the Prince, Achille Fould, Maximilien Koenigswarter and the adventurous Duke of Brunswick advanced large sums of money. To her friend, Alfred d'Orsay, Miss Howard wrote that she was throwing everything she possessed into the fray. It is certain that at this time with her passion for conspiracy she mortgaged her London houses, sold her saddle-horses and pawned all her jewels. "The Prince was wrong to accept this sacrifice," wrote Fleury; "by not refusing her, he contracted serious obligations. The mistress had the better role . . ." [1]

Where did Harriet acquire "rights and interests in the domain of Civita Nova, on the borders of Ancona, in the Papal States"? This is a mystery which has not been cleared up. Nevertheless, in 1848 she had made these lands over to Louis Napoleon for three millions, payable in 1851 only. The Prince thereupon raised three hundred and twenty-four thousand francs in cash from the Marquis Pallavicino on a first mortgage on Civita Nova, a property which he himself had just acquired on credit. "The form the operation took saved appearances," wrote Adrien Dansette. But, in 1851, having bills protested by Montaut, a money-changer at the Palais-Royal, Harriet Howard paid his debts without any further regard to appearances.[2]

She was bent on self-abnegation. When, a few days before the *coup d'état*, there was a deficiency of liquid cash, it was again Miss Howard who gave the Prince two hundred thousand gold

---

[1] *Souvenirs du général comte Fleury*, Vol. I, p. 206.

[2] *Papiers et Correspondance de la famille impériale*, Vol. I, p. 170. (Paris, Imprimerie nationale, 3 vol. octavo, 1870-72).

francs *in specie* (equivalent to forty thousand pounds sterling to-day).

The 2nd December, the anniversary of Austerlitz and of Napoleon's coronation, was a day of triumph. The deputies, " arrested in their beds," were in prison, the Assembly dissolved and the rebels condemned to be deported. The footmen of the Élysée were wearing an Imperial livery identical to that worn at the Tuileries by the uncle's servants. These green liveries had been ordered and even delivered months before. The permanent President was to be served by an Imperial household.

" The man of Providence," who believed himself created by the God of armies to rule over France, had at last reached the goal he had pursued since the Strasbourg escapade. How did Harriet, even in her radiant and ingenuous happiness, fail to understand that a Prince, even more than a President, was rising too high for her to follow his vertiginous ascent?

*   *   *

At twenty-seven years of age General Bonaparte had married Josephine whose lover he was. But the Emperor Napoleon, in his forties, had repudiated her in order to form a union with an Archduchess of Hapsburg blood. Elected by a young Republic for a term of office which was to last only four years and which could not be renewed, Louis Napoleon in 1848 could have regularised his union with a woman who was, in her devotion, sublime. He might even have done so out of gratitude, if Harriet had then been pregnant. But like Josephine, who by her first marriage was the mother of Eugène and Hortense, and then, upon marrying a second time at the age of thirty-three, had failed to produce an heir to the throne, Miss Howard who, while still quite young, had conceived a child in sin, had thereafter remained barren. But now, the change in the régime was necessarily to imply a return to the hereditary dynastic principle.

To all intents and purposes the Empire had been re-created.

The Prince-President decided to wait for the following 2nd December (a day of good augury) to change his title but, throughout the year 1852, he nevertheless acted as sovereign. From the Élysée, the presidential palace, he moved into the Tuileries, a royal residence. The 15th August, Napoleon's birthday, which under the Empire had been France's national holiday, was reinstated. The civil code was once more known by the magic name of the Code Napoléon. Eagles reappeared upon the flagstaffs, which until then had been surmounted by a pike. The coins struck by the Mint still bore on the reverse the words *République française*, but on the obverse a profile with a little pointed beard and the inscription: *Louis Bonaparte*.

The King of Rome, who had died abroad as the Duke of Reichstadt, had never reigned. From a sort of fictional courtesy, Prince Louis turned L'Aiglon into a posthumous Emperor: Napoleon II. He himself took the figure III.

After him, who would inherit the throne? His nearest relation, his first cousin, the brother of Mathilde, would take rank as the presumptive heir, but that particular Napoleon was a left-wing Prince, turbulent and subversive. To prevent his inheriting the throne appeared a duty. The idea of marriage, therefore, became a necessity in her lover's mind, though in a form quite contrary to the wishes of Miss Howard.

An Emperor actually in power could undoubtedly marry into a ruling family. Not so long ago the King of Bavaria, the King of Wurtemberg and the Emperor of Austria had wed their daughters to his own uncles: Eugène de Beauharnais, Jerome Bonaparte and Napoleon. With surprising promptness he sent Fleury to Darmstadt to negotiate a marriage with Caroline Wasa, granddaughter of the late King of Sweden, Gustav IV, and of the Dowager Grand-Duchess of Baden. But an earlier suitor for her hand, the hereditary Prince of Saxe, had already succeeded in pleasing and was chosen. Checkmate for Bonaparte.

Disappointed, the latter commissioned his cousin Walewski, French Ambassador in London, to ask the Foreign Office if a niece of the Queen of England, Adelaide of Hohenlohe, then aged sixteen, would be granted him? The Duchess of Kent, mother of Queen Victoria, had had, by a first marriage, an elder daughter, Theodora of Leiningen who, having become Princess of Hohenlohe, had made her the grandmother of this eminently eligible girl. At that time all the Courts of Europe treated Louis Napoleon as an adventurer. He knew it well but did not think that he was aiming too high in asking from her Britannic Majesty a half-niece. What he did not know, was that Lord Normanby, in his reports to the Foreign Office, continued to represent him as a sentimental lover, devoted to Miss Howard and secretly determined to marry her. The English diplomat was determined to be romantic, that is to say to support the pretensions of the Emperor's mistress. It was an error of judgment which cost him his post for, at about this time, he lost the Paris Embassy and was sent in disgrace as Minister to Florence, at that time the capital of the Grand Duchy of Tuscany. Queen Victoria, however, indicated that the parents of Princess Adelaide were alone in a position to dispose of her hand and that they must be asked according to the proper forms of protocol. The Hohenlohe-Langenbergs, as Lutheran Princes, were devoutly Protestant. They replied that the difference of religion constituted a major obstacle and that their daughter, Adelaide, refused to make a mixed marriage. A second checkmate for Bonaparte.

Journal de Viel-Castel, 18th August, 1852: At the ball at Saint-Cloud, the President was preoccupied. Miss Howard, his mistress, had been in the house since morning and, as she had been absent because of the marriage negotiations, her return was in a sense a reconciliation. For half an hour, at about half-past ten, the Prince retired with her to *rest*. He finally retired at one o'clock.[1]

[1] *Mémoires du comte Horace de Viel-Castel*, Vol. II, p. 96.

Viel-Castel was not the only one to note Harriet's victorious return:

" His mistress's ambitions have grown greater with events," wrote Fleury . . . " A woman like her, of quite exceptional beauty, beloved, intelligent, might well aspire to the highest position . . . By the mere fact that she had given proofs of devotion, she had the right to expect the rewards of her clever generosity . . ."

The same observer added later:

" Though our relations with Miss Howard were extremely pleasant, though she never departed from a manner of almost deferential politeness towards us, her attitude had slightly changed. She had become more exacting with regard to ceremonies and excursions and had now lost some of her accustomed reserve . . . If military reviews took place at Versailles, she no longer stood some distance off, lost in the crowd. A special place had to be found for her, well in the public view . . ."[1]

Harriet, having survived two crises, thought herself invulnerable.

One night, at Saint-Cloud, the Prince, in the madness of their mutual passion, took what she always called " the holy oath." To the end of her life, she maintained that it was a promise of marriage. In this she was mistaken. In their tender correspondence, the Frenchman, loved by a foreigner, discreetly measured his words. By writing that he meant " to do something to make her happy " (*faire le bonheur*) he meant that he would restore her financial situation. By writing that he intended to " raise her to the position she deserved " (*la mettre enfin à sa vraie place*) he meant that he would ennoble her by Imperial edict. By " tightening such dear links " (*resserrer des liens si chers*), he intended to indicate that a marriage for reasons of state implied no break in their relationship which he looked upon as indissoluble. The idea, frequently expressed, that " separation was inconceivable " (*la séparation serait inconcevable*) meant, at the most, an assurance that she would not be exiled. Once

---

[1] *Souvenirs du général comte Fleury*, Vol. I, p. 208-9.

married, the Emperor intended to take no steps to banish Miss Howard. Subtle and reticent as he was, he swore fidelity to his mistress in the same degree that he had sworn to observe the constitution of the republic.

Journal de Viel-Castel, 30th October, 1852: The day before yesterday, at the Opera, there was a Gala night attended by the President. Ovations, applause, acclamations . . . The public, full of goodwill as it is, was upset by seeing in a grand box, and covered with diamonds, Mme Howard, the President's mistress; this makes a bad impression. Prince Jérôme had his mistress with him in his box. We know rather too much about this business of mistresses; it's out of date . . . The President's circle is detestable . . .[1]

The elevation of the Prince to the throne was, necessarily, to increase the distance he must keep between himself and others. Afraid of losing ground, Harriet wished at least to occupy firmly the terrain already ceded. The Englishwoman, who until now had kept herself discreetly in the background, took a pathetic pleasure in making a parade of herself in public. She was surrounded, supported and encouraged by a faithful group: the Comte de Toulongeon, *aide-de-camp* to the Prince-President, Edgar Ney, Persigny, Colonel the Comte de Béville, Doctor Conneau, Comte Bacciochi, the Marquess of Hertford, the Mocquard family, Doctor Evans and a ghost from St. Helena, old General de Montholon.

On the 2nd December everything went according to plan. The result of the plebiscite was 7,824,189 for, as opposed to 253,145 against. The Emperor made his entry into Paris to the sound of guns and bells. The following evening at the Tuileries, there was a banquet and a reception for the diplomatic corps.

Journal de Viel-Castel, 3rd December, 1852: The Emperor said to Princesse Mathilde: " My dear Mathilde, until there is an Empress, you take precedence here and will always sit on my right." Will

[1] *Mémoires du comte Horace de Viel-Castel*, Vol. II, p. 110.

there be an Empress?... Miss Harriet Howard flatters herself
that she will prevent the Emperor marrying...[1]

Between Madame his Concubine and Madame his Cousin, a
cold war had been going on for four years. "It's the battle of
the heart of gold against the heart of stone," said Mocquard
compassionately. The intransigent hardness of Princesse Mathilde
was a reef against which the ship carrying Harriet and her
fortunes must, sooner or later, be wrecked. When the two
women met, in the passages or gardens of the Château of
Saint-Cloud, Miss Howard made a deep curtsey; Her Imperial
Highness barely acknowledged the salutation and went on
her way, exchanging an ironical smile with her lady-in-
waiting.

Napoleon III, more sensual than affectionate, "loved women
too much to love one only." Since he had become the master
of France, many beautiful and ambitious women had offered
themselves to him. Harriet was no longer the sole object of his
desires. "The Rue du Cirque, so close to the Elysée, does not
lead to the Tuileries!" she sighed. Already the favourite's
drawing-room lacked the presence of certain adventurers, who
had come there in the past only because they were certain of
meeting her protector in intimate surroundings.

Her true and enduring love was the redemption of a good-
hearted girl. She had long hoped that marriage would be her
rehabilitation. But when the professions of Saint-Cloud were
not followed by public action, Harriet had resigned herself to
losing the Emperor in order to keep the lover. She admitted
that he preserved her pride in asking for the hands of distant
princesses by proxy. But, set aside from the throne, she nevertheless did not wish to be turned out of the imperial palaces and
desired to maintain her rank of permanent mistress at the new
Court.

It is to be remembered that Jeanne Bécu, called Vaubernier,

[1] *Mémoires du comte Horace de Viel-Castel*, Vol. II, p. 125.

the favourite of Louis XV and married to a complaisant husband, had wished to be publicly received at Versailles. Etiquette required that a great lady, who already had the entrée, should be responsible for the candidate, leading her forward to make her three curtseys to the Sovereigns. To please the King, the Comtesse de Béarn had agreed to play this role of godmother and the official presentation of the recently created Comtesse du Barry had gone off without incident and with the customary ceremonial.

In the same way, Harriet Howard wished, in order to reaffirm her tottering power, to assert her privileges. A Court ball was to be given at the Tuileries. Protocol sent out to the several thousands who had the right to it the invitation cards with the arms of the Emperor, and the head of Protocol was Félix Bacciochi, first Chamberlain, and the introducer of ambassadors to the presence.

Miss Howard, who only saw the sovereign in private, never being invited to official dinner-parties, pretended to believe that, having the right of entry to the palace by secret doors and back staircases, she was to all intents and purposes at home and could appear in the gallery des Maréchaux during an evening party.

"How astonished we were," wrote Fleury, "when we saw Miss Howard appear on the arm of Colonel de Béville, whom she has won over to her cause, escorted by Comte Bacciochi and preceded by a lady of her circle who was, in these circumstances, playing the part of the Comtesse de Béarn! In an elegant gown, her appearance radiant, her head resembling an antique cameo, with her tall figure and her duchess-like manner, she, who was soon to call herself the Comtesse de Beauregard de Béchevêt, was remarked for her incomparable beauty. Unknown to most of those present, she was fortunately taken for a lady lately arrived from London in order to attend a friend's ball. But from that night on, Miss Howard appeared in her true colours: those of a great courtesan whose ambitious projects must, at all costs, be frustrated . . . The bad impression created by the royal mistress's appearance was courageously noted in the Prefect of Police's report.[1] It was a weapon in our hands ... It had to be cleverly used. I undertook this task ..." [2]

There were now so many people leagued against Harriet that her final defeat was inevitable.

[1] Charlemagne-Émile de Maupas (1818–88).
[2] *Souvenirs du général comte Fleury*, Vol. I, p. 209-10.

CHAPTER FIVE

THE WISE VIRGIN

PRINCESSE MATHILDE had no wish for the Emperor to marry for she enjoyed performing the functions of an Empress at Court, knowing that, if Napoleon III should die a bachelor, her own brother would succeed to the throne. What she could not forgive the Sovereign was " to be in love with a woman of low extraction." By her mother, Catherine of Würtemburg, Princesse Mathilde was the granddaughter of a king and the niece of the Czar. A " creature " who had lost caste, who was decried and discussed, filled her with horror.

She would have liked the Emperor to have a mistress of her finding, one who was well connected and well brought up and would listen to the advice of " Madame Cousine," one who would create no embarrassment and might even be useful. There seemed to her to be no other way of breaking " the English chain."

Mathilde Bonaparte was a blue-stocking who, in her house in the Rue de Courcelles, gave one dinner to writers and another to painters every week. As far as her own inclinations were concerned, she would have preferred to be surrounded only with artists and intellectuals. But, for some time past, she had invited fashionable women, who were considered " fast," to her receptions; she even asked up from their country houses a few pretty girls without portions or expectations, who might be tempted into an adventure with Jupiter.

The Prince was still President when one night, at an intimate dinner party, she had presented to him a fair traveller who was passing through Paris. The new arrival, who was escorted everywhere by her mother, was creating a sensation. She was a fair Spaniard, a rare combination, and all the more attractive thereby. She had been invited to the Élysée, then to Saint-Cloud, and later to hunt at Fontainebleau, for she was said to be a fearless horsewoman. She was only three years younger than the favourite, but had the triple advantage over Miss Howard of being a Grandee of Spain, a sister of the Duchess of Alba, and a virgin. Without fortune and much courted, she wished to be respectable and cleverly made a virtue of frigidity. She was twenty-six years old and her name was Eugenia de Montijo.

Her history in short was this: her father, Don Cypriano, had served in the Grand Army and lost an eye on the field of honour. Her mother, Doña Manuela, who had formerly been a friend of Stendhal's, corresponded with Prosper Mérimée. She herself had received a completely French education at the Convent of the Sacred Heart in the Rue de Varenne.

In 1844 the Duke of Alba having hesitated for some time between the Montijo sisters, had chosen Paca, a classic brunette with dark eyes. Eugenia had been much upset. For eight years, dragging the old Comtesse in her wake, from Spain to England and from France to Germany, she had sought to make a marriage out of vexation which would be also one of revenge. To go one better than the duchies of Alba and Berwick, the blood of the Stuart kings and the twelve grandeeships of the first class, she required at least the distinctions of a mediatised prince. For lack of such a suitor for her hand, Eugenia had remained single.

She had so great a success in Paris that her prolonged spinsterhood appeared inexplicable. It was said that an unrequited youthful love had permanently affected her; but the witnesses to the period of her adolescence were not in accord upon the supposed object of this incurable passion; some said the Duke of Alba; others, the Duke of Sesto.

The Emperor, who was extremely responsive to beauty in young women, endeavoured to seduce her. He laid siege to her with both heat and precipitation. He met a firm resistance which was a nicely balanced mixture of affronted modesty, Castilian dignity and bewitching coquetry. To repel such an abruptness of attack, Doña Eugenia was possessed of a fierce pride and a capacity for wit. Having read Victor Hugo, long before the poet went into exile, she had the courage to quote *Hernani*:

> Mon vieux père a pour vous versé son sang à flots.
> Moi, je suis fille noble et, de ce sang jalouse,
> Trop pour la favorite et trop peu pour l'épouse! . . .

One day, at Compiègne, leaning on the window-sill of her room, she allowed Romeo Bonaparte to play Shakespeare's balcony scene:

" How do I reach you? " he sighed. " Where lies the road that leads to your heart? "

" By the church, sire," replied the Spanish Juliet.

The skirmish resulted in nothing. So, in order to put an end to these compromising attentions, the señorita left for Madrid. She spent the summer of 1852 taking the waters at Baden. A few letters of loving friendship passed between pursuer and pursued. Those of Eugenia, well-written, even rather too well-written, had been revised and corrected in draft by Mérimée.

The determination with which Miss Howard had imposed herself upon the Court had displeased the master of the Tuileries. Allusions reminding him of the " oath of Saint-Cloud " irritated him still more. Snubbed, Harriet became plaintive. The sacrifice of her wealth, and six years of humiliation, stoically borne in a false position, certainly militated in her favour. But she was wrong to allude to them at a moment of crisis. The Emperor was physically in love with her and, in his own words, " always returned to her with pleasure "; a tearful mistress bored him.

After a long absence, the Montijos, mother and daughter, returned to their old quarters in Paris of the previous autumn, the Hôtel du Rhin, 6 Place Vendôme. Their return coincided with the definite refusal of the hand of Princess Adelaide of Hohenlohe, who was too attached to the Confession of Augsburg to marry a Papist Sovereign. Mlle de Montijo could be seen hunting at Compiègne on a superb chestnut horse. Without departing for an instant from her inflexible chastity, she became, so it seemed, sufficiently human for the Emperor to offer her the horse she had been riding. To a young Spanish diplomat,[1] younger brother of the Duke of Alba, Eugenia wrote: " *Querido Enrique: no te puedes figurar lo q. dicen de mi por haber aceptado el dichoso caballo!* . . . Dear Enrique, you cannot believe what is said of me for having accepted this damned horse! . . ."[2] But to the pure all things are pure, and *honi soit qui mal y pense.*

After the horse, the fair one received from her lover a jewel in the form of a clover-leaf, whose petals were four emeralds spread wide in a dew of brilliants. Presents multiplied, but Miss Howard had not been discarded and the word " marriage " had not been mentioned.

Two utterly dissimilar foreigners were competing in a game for which the Crown of France was the stake. The woman who loved had already risked more than she could afford to lose: heart and soul, body and goods. The wise virgin was aflame with pure ambition and conserved her trumps.

Without naming either the Spaniard or the Englishwoman, Arsène Houssaye wrote their story in the Chinese manner. In this transparent piece of fiction, Napoleon III is supposed to be reigning over the Celestial Empire:

The son of Heaven was fond of women. Some of his courtiers feared that he would be dominated by an ancient mistress; she was

[1] Don Enrique-Luis Fitzjames Stuart, Count of Galve (1826–82).
[2] *Lettres de l'impératrice Eugénie,* edited by the seventeenth Duke of Alba (her great-nephew) in 1935, p. 44.

an extremely beautiful creature who had come from a northern country ... but some other of the Emperor's courtiers, fascinated by this bewitching creature, worked in the dark to make of her, who knows what?—perhaps an Empress.

That is why she was one day seen to appear at a court reception, to the great surprise of the Emperor himself ... She was, moreover, escorted by those courtiers who wished to raise her to the throne; they had even dared give her two ladies-in-waiting. This apparition was like a flash of lightning in a rose garden.

The transposition does not extend to all the characters in the story; that representing Mérimée is called " the Academician," not " the Mandarin." According to Houssaye, the Emperor's marriage was the rose-tinted climax to a three years' sentimental progress, composed and staged by the author of *Carmen*:

The Academician wished to plan a novel in real life. Would it not be much more amusing than to take pen in hand? He had under his hand two foreigners, a mother and daughter, two real romantic heroines ... Jealous people did not hesitate to say that both mother and daughter were mere adventuresses without resources, who were spending their last maravedi upon their appearance. How was the novelist to present his heroine so that she might take the eye of the Emperor of China?

It was autumn, the hunting season. The novelist said to the minister, " The mother and daughter must be invited. The mother will stay in the Summer Palace; the daughter will go hunting."

The daughter was adorably beautiful ... One might have thought her Diana the Huntress, with Venus's smile. The Emperor nearly lost his stirrups at sight of her ...

The next day, the Emperor of China, who had slept badly, appeared most melancholy. The fact was that the girl—who had promised the novelist to obey him, so that the play might achieve a fitting climax—had left by the first caravan ...

The fantastic Chinese story hardly deviates from reality. Houssaye, familiar with the circle he was describing, was very well informed. After having told the story of the flight to Madrid, he wrote:

When the girl had left, the monarch was more lonely than ever. He thought of summoning his mistress, but the face which had once been his passion no longer meant anything to him now; the new one had killed the old . . .[1]

Harriet, abandoned and offended, then committed the imprudence of claiming to be a privileged creditor of the régime. The Emperor owed her five million gold francs. With extraordinary stupidity, she dared remind him of it. All scruples gone, Napoleon III came to the conclusion that it was less a question of crushing a broken heart than of settling a debt.

Miss Howard had in her possession receipts signed by his hand. She could have confounded those who accused her of doing the Emperor harm by demonstrating that Cæsar was under an obligation towards her, since she had given him very considerable sums of money. She preserved in the Rue du Cirque, with the irrefutable proofs of his being her debtor, an extensive correspondence, collected into bundles and symbolically tied with the thin silk ribbon known as a " favour."

There were no telephones at that time. The least suspicion of a sentimental attachment left behind it some trace in manuscript. Harriet, now abandoned, sadly went over the relics of the past: English letters from the exiled gaol-breaker, political letters from the Pretender, love-letters, declarations of political principle, professions of faith, bulletins of victory, projects for a joint future, plans for constitutional reform—then, alas, communications of decreasing length: plans postponed, meetings cancelled; the successive episodes of a love story implicit in the contemporary chapters of a History of France.

Napoleon III knew that, in England, the breach of a promise to marry was a crime. Both before and after Saint-Cloud, he had so often answered his mistress's anxious prayers with reassuring words, that he was no longer certain he had not made

[1] Arsène Houssaye, *Les Trois Rayonnantes*, p. 203–8.

her written promises. He attached no importance to them, nor did he consider them an engagement. But his reservations had been mental ones. What would a lawyer think of his written words? In this month of December 1852 the Emperor, utterly preoccupied with his new passion, blamed himself for having written so often to his mistress, day after day, during the last six years! How could he recover from Miss Howard the treasures to which the Englishwoman, Victorian and sentimental as she was, so passionately adhered?

Did he for one moment suppose that she was capable of bringing against him a breach of promise case in the country of her birth? Nothing in her past behaviour could warrant such a suspicion. However, the Emperor, always wary, took fright. Incapable of weighing the respective merits of the two women between whom his inconstant heart had for so long been held in suspense, he feared that Harriet would throw the weight of her papers into the balance.

He was, in fact, wrong. No unpleasant revelations ever threatened Eugenia de Montijo's calm serenity. Her rival, tortured with jealousy as she was, was nevertheless incapable of such vulgarity. Two adversaries, equal in pride and beauty, confronted each other, observed each other—and ignored each other.

Out of favour, Miss Howard wrote to a compatriot:

"His Majesty was here last night, offering to pay me off; yes, an earldom in my own right, a castle, and a decent French husband into the bargain ... Oh! the pity of it all! I could put up with a dose of laudanum ... The Lord Almighty spent two hours arguing with me ... Later, he fell asleep on the crimson sofa and snored while I wept ..." [1]

Loved by Harriet Howard, the "squat little man with bow legs," whom Mérimée called the *Dynast*, was in love with a virgin from Castile. Would he add this splendid quarry to his game

[1] Unpublished letter in a private collection.

book? Bets were being laid at the Tuileries. The Austro-Hungarian Ambassador wondered "when the walls would be breached and when the fortress would surrender?" Their Imperial Highnesses and the Courtiers believed they were watching the preliminaries to a liaison, not the preparations for a misalliance. The latter would create in Europe so much political inconvenience that the ministers were violently opposed to it. Lord Cowley, who had succeeded Lord Normanby as British Ambassador in Paris, wrote to the Foreign Secretary:

"Mrs. H[oward] is, I believe, at last *congédiée* . . . The Emperor's entourage is getting seriously alarmed at his admiration of a certain Spanish young lady, Mademoiselle de Montijo by name. Her mother is, with the young lady, playing a bold game, and, I cannot doubt, hopes that her daughter may wear the Imperial Crown. Some of the Emperor's friends are not without apprehension that she may succeed in her intrigues, and St. Arnaud, the Minister of War, has spoken very openly and strongly to the Emperor on the subject; as if a man in love ever listened to reason! The Emperor thanked him for his advice and said nothing more, and his attentions to the young lady have been more marked ever since . . ."

Another letter: "The Emperor is going it finely with the young Montijo . . . He is so extraordinary a man that he will set everything at defiance, if it so pleases him." [1]

Miss Howard had her spies in the Palace and they kept her informed as to the doings of the enemy. While Prince Napoleon said: "One can [love] Mlle de Montijo; one cannot marry her," Harriet, a better psychologist, was writing to her English confidante: "If the fair Infanta has not yielded, marry he may . . ." This was also the opinion of the charming Marquise de Contades who, at about this time, wrote to her father, the Maréchal de Castellane:

[1] *The Paris Embassy during the Second Empire, selections from the papers of Henry Richard Charles Wellesley, first Earl of Cowley, edited by his son, Colonel the Hon. F. A. Wellesley,* p. 14–15.

"Nothing is talked of here but the marriage of the Emperor with Mlle de Montijo. Well, between ourselves, it could happen. The Emperor has fallen very much in love with her ... From the political point of view, the marriage has a certain inconvenience, but if it does not take place, it is more than likely that the Emperor will not marry at all. Old ' English chains,' who are still very close to him and are the terror of those who love him, may hold him back ..."[1]

Eugenia's main fault was pride; a devouring pride, an infernal passion which stifled every emotion. At twenty-seven, she was a fine young woman who was beginning to turn into a confirmed spinster. Nevertheless, she was resigned to taking the veil rather than fall below the level of her sister Paca, Duchess of Alba and Berwick. Her arrogant obstinacy was to lead her to Notre-Dame de Paris:

"She will marry the Emperor. He loves her. She does not love him ... He is much older than she is, but old husbands are the most attentive. Moreover, he is the Emperor. Since she has no portion and is surrounded with perils in which her reputation is suffering a decline, she must marry. Well, she will! ... Her marriage will be a fairy-tale marriage, a marriage the whole world will talk of ... She will try to be useful to the country over which she is to reign. For a proud and active nature, this may amount to a kind of happiness ..."[2]

Too frank to feign emotions she did not feel, she replied to his ardent proposals by declaring her indifference. Let the monarch decide. Eugenia is worth a wedding mass. He is tempted, but still very hesitant. "The difficulty with the Emperor," said Morny, "is to remove a fixed idea from his mind and to give him firmness of will."

Napoleon III was forty-five, but he seemed older. The beautiful Spaniard was ready to swear obedience and loyalty to

[1] Letter published by the Maréchal de Castellane in his *Journal*, Vol. IV, p. 423.
[2] Octave Aubry, *L'Impératrice Eugénie*, p. 82-3.

him; she could not promise to love him with passion. He always intimidated her and sometimes irritated her. For instance, the name she had received at her baptism was pronounced " Ourenia " in Spanish. When the Emperor called her "Ugénie," the young woman thought his pronunciation vulgar; she could not accustom herself to it.

CHAPTER SIX

WEDDING MARCH

THE PRINCESSES BONAPARTE and the other ladies of the Palace were offended at seeing a foreigner, without diplomatic or official status, taking too prominent a place at Court. As she passed by, derogatory remarks were apt to be made until finally the peculiar insolence of two elderly ladies was to precipitate events. On the 31st December, 1852, Doña Manuela and her daughter were invited to a New Year's Eve dinner by the Emperor. Doña Eugenia, a Grandee of Spain, thought that a foreigner of rank took precedence over the wife of a French Minister. At the moment when the guests were forming procession to go into dinner, two by two, the "little Montijo" took precedence over Mme Fortoul, the wife of the Minister of Education. The latter indignantly snubbed her, calling her an adventuress. Eugenia, pale as a lily in her white satin gown, replied coldly: "Lead on, Madame." After dinner, she told the Emperor that she had been insulted in his house. Not being a woman to stand further similar affronts, she would leave France for ever. Honour was not to be trifled with. He promised to marry her, before God and his ministers.

Having promised, he asked for a postponement. He must have time to inform his relations, get rid of his mistress and receive in private single audience the members of his cabinet. They all expected him to marry into "the family of kings." Uncles, cousins, secretaries of state, would all unanimously blame him for marrying out of inclination. The Dynast would have to convince them of the excellence of his choice. As for Miss Howard, said the Emperor, she was a very old friend (she was twenty-nine), much impoverished (he did not mention why), who had for a long time past been resigned to living in retirement. To break this " English chain," now so lacking in money, it would be sufficient to heap gold upon her, and load her with heraldic trinkets. Harriet, once endowed, would be created a comtesse by a territorial title. With her son, and for the child's sake, the now repentant woman would take up her residence in the country. Was not the first duty of the territorial nobility to reside upon its land? In the provinces a title covers a multitude of sins. The Emperor's old mistress would vanish, like the year 1852, at the first stroke of midnight ... Come to the mistletoe, here's the New Year! Make way for the Emperor's fiancée.

1st January, 1853 ... Doña Manuela expected the Emperor of the French to come to her, incognito, to present his usual good wishes and ask for her daughter's hand. Nothing happened on that first day. Nor did it upon the morrow. Nothing had even happened by the 3rd January. What were they to do? The Montijo ladies held a council at the Hôtel du Rhin with their cousin Ferdinand de Lesseps and Prosper Mérimée. The young Count of Galve was present and consulted. His elder brother, the Duke of Alba, had had him appointed to the Spanish Legation in Paris in order that, at balls, hunting parties and during games of hide-and-seek, the wise virgin should have a bodyguard, always ready to intervene should the Imperial faun attempt her virtue. The Duke of Alba feared for the honour of his family. He expected no glorious results from the excessive ambitions of the two visionary women and prayed his sister-in-law not to allow herself to be compromised.

Mérimée reasoned as a cynic, Lesseps as a visionary, Galve as a *caballero*. What was the matter under discussion? It was to determine whether Eugenia could, without loss of

prestige, wait beneath the Vendôme column for the Emperor,
so eternally indecisive, to come and place the ring upon her
finger.

Why did he preserve so complete a silence? Had he even
started the promised negotiations? Lacking all news from him,
Eugenia thought that the battle was lost and suggested a tactical
retreat. She prayed her mother to leave at once for Rome. The
Comtesse was of a contrary opinion: a sudden departure, she
said decisively, would be called a rout. Galve appealed to
Castilian honour; Lesseps spoke convincingly of the unexpected-
ness of love; Mérimée expressed the fear that Miss Howard had
recaptured the impetuous Napoleon III by mere physical attrac-
tion.

They were still discussing the matter when a courier on horseback arrived at the Hôtel du Rhin with a message, sealed with
the Imperial arms. Was it the communication they were waiting
for? Not at all. It was no more than an invitation to a Court
Ball on 12th January.

The discussion among the five of them continued. What
weight were they to attach to this piece of pasteboard? Was it
the gesture of a persistent lover or merely a routine piece of
protocol? ... Everyone knows that the invitations of a Sovereign are commands. Doña Manuela, once *camarera mayor* to
Isabelle II, was naturally much in favour of obeying the laws of
etiquette. Lesseps, for his part, maintained that the daughter of
a noble family who was without fear or reproach, must not give
way before the wife of a minister. This appeal to pride provoked
a sudden change of mind in Eugenia. Very well; she would go
to the Tuileries in a new dress and for the last time. There,
Bérénice would bid a superb and memorable farewell to the
weak Emperor.

The ball was at its height when the Spaniard, dressed in ivory
brocade trimmed with silver tassels, made her entry on the arm
of Baron James de Rothschild. She saluted the Emperor with
a deep curtsey as he sat on the dais. Then, somewhat confused,

she tried to find a seat. All those allotted to ordinary mortals being already taken, Mlle de Montijo moved towards the privileged zone which lay on the Emperor's left. Mme Drouyn de Lhuys, the wife of the Minister for Foreign Affairs, strongly defended her settee against the Spanish invasion. Eugenia and the elderly Countess were sharply and angrily rebuffed. Cæsar, seeing the insult from afar, asked the Montijo ladies to come up on to the dais and take their place among the Princes of the Blood. Later, having opened the ball with the British Ambassadress, Lady Cowley, he sent the Master of Ceremonies to Doña Eugenia to invite the victim of the privileged to dance a quadrille with His Majesty himself.

As soon as she had taken the Emperor's arm she reproached him with his evasive and elusive attitude. He hadn't by any chance forgotten to marry her, had he? When the band stopped playing, she asked for an immediate audience with the Sovereign. Did he not owe her at least an explanation? Had she not innocently trusted the word of a Bonaparte? And now she was being treated everywhere as a rejected adventuress! Much moved, the Emperor led her into the Louis XIV drawing-room which he used as his study at the Tuileries. After the private audience, which was much remarked upon at the time, Jean Mocquard was urgently summoned to His Majesty's presence. Napoleon III had an open letter in his hand which he gave to his *cnef de cabinet*.

" Monsieur," the Emperor said, " pray seal this letter and take it yourself to-morrow morning to the Place Vendôme to Madame la Comtesse de Montijo." [1]

Here is the text of the historic letter. Aubry, Dansette and Treich have quoted it.

Palais des Tuileries, 15th January, 1853

MADAME LA COMTESSE,

For a long time I have been in love with Mademoiselle your daughter and have wished to make her my wife. I am to-day,

---

[1] Octave Aubry, *L'Impératrice Eugénie*, p. 95.

therefore, asking you for her hand, for there is no one so capable of making my happiness or more worthy to wear a crown.

I pray you, if you consent to this proposal, not to reveal it till we have been able to make our arrangements.

Believe me, Madame la Comtesse, when I assure you of my sincere friendship.

NAPOLEON

After two years of uncertainty, the Emperor, having at last made up his mind, seemed to want to rush to the altar. The reply to the letter Mocquard brought being, naturally, in the affirmative, Achille Fould then visited Doña Manuela. He came officially, in his capacity of Minister of State, to ask for the hand of Eugenia de Montijo in the name of the Emperor. The maternal consent was given there and then. The Emperor decided that their engagement should be announced to the French people on the 22nd January. The civil marriage was fixed for the 29th; the religious ceremony for the 30th. This was hurrying things on with a vengeance.

Eugenia de Montijo to the Duchess of Alba: My dear good sister, I wish to be the first to inform you of my marriage with the Emperor . . . He has fought and won. The Ministers have agreed. He will announce it to the Chamber in the speech from the throne . . . He would be happy if you could be present, but it seems to me impossible in view of the short time . . . Destiny, which has linked us since childhood, seems now about to separate us, but I hope that you will come from time to time to bask in my affection, which will always remain unaltered and sincere . . . Please do not say anything about it for the moment, in order to avoid anonymous letters . . .

Be kind enough to buy me two scarlet fans, the finest you can find; if none please you, send as far as Cadiz in search of them. Please try to find another of sandalwood with silver filigree, and another one gilded, the most elegant that you can lay your hands on . . . I would also like a pretty Andalusian *moña*; I need it for a fancy dress ball. It must be very light and very pretty . . . I am sending you for your birthday a charming mantle from Madame

Doucet . . . I am very busy. Good-bye. I am sending you a copy of His Majesty's letter (here follows Napoleon III's letter to Doña Manuela quoted above).[1]

Lord Cowley, the British Ambassador, announced the engagement to Lord John Russell, the Foreign Secretary, in contemptuous terms:

"We are living in a society of adventurers. The great one of all has been captured by an adventuress. To hear the way men and women talk of their future Empress is astounding. Things have been repeated to me, which the Emperor has said of her, and others which have been said to him, which it would be impossible to commit to paper. In fact, she has played her game with him so well, that he can get her in no other way but marriage, and it is to gratify his passions that he marries her . . ."

Answer of Lord John Russell to Lord Cowley: "A marriage with a well-behaved young Frenchwoman would, I think, have been very politic, but to put this *intrigante* on the throne is a lowering of the Imperial dignity with a vengeance!"[2]

Napoleon III was marrying a girl without a dowry. He arranged an income for the future Empress of two hundred and fifty thousand francs and gave her unlimited credit for the purpose of buying her trousseau. Already the great dressmakers had obtained permission for the major articles of this fairy-like trousseau to be shown in their shop windows in the Rue de la Paix. Doña Manuela, who lived by borrowing money from her son-in-law the Duke of Alba, *querido Jimy*, wept with relief when she heard from the Imperial lawyers that she was not to be asked to put up a penny. The whole inheritance derived from the late Count of Montijo had been dispersed in travelling and hotel

---

[1] *Lettres familières de l'impératrice Eugénie* published by the Duke of Alba, with the assistance of F. de Llanos y Torriglia and of Pierre Josserand, Vol. I, p. 47–9.

[2] *The Paris Embassy during the Second Empire,* the papers of Lord Cowley, edited by his son. p. 17.

expenses by his sixty-year-old widow. It was high time that their younger daughter should make a good marriage.

A few hours before the unforgettable visit of Achille Fould, a dun had come to the Hôtel du Rhin with a writ. At the request of a dressmaker, Mme Barenne, the government official summoned the Comtesse de Montijo to meet a whole pile of unpaid bills.

Eugenia de Montijo to the Duchess of Alba, 22nd January, 1853: This is a sad time. I am saying farewell to my family and my country, in order to devote myself exclusively to the man who has loved me sufficiently to raise me up to his throne ... I fear the responsibilities that will weigh upon me, and yet I am accomplishing my destiny. I am afraid, not of assassins, but to appear in history as a lesser woman than Blanche de Castile and Anne of Austria ...

On the eve of mounting one of the greatest thrones in Europe, I cannot prevent myself feeling a certain terror: the responsibility is enormous ... I have accepted this greatness as a divine mission ... I have suffered much in my life; my faith in happiness was almost extinguished. Well, now, I believe in it. I was so little accustomed to being loved! My life was a huge desert ... When, tired of life, I chanced to find some kind of affection, I was only loved superficially and came out of it in despair. This man has an irresistible strength of will ... He was prepared to hazard his crown in order to share it with me. He has no hesitations: he is always prepared to stake his future on the turn of a card; that is why he always wins ... Papa said to me one day when we were talking politics: "*Las mujeres a hacer calcetas* ... women are for knitting stockings!" I knew very well that I was not destined for that! ... I have a feeling that I shall be able to be useful to my country ... Soon I shall be alone here and friendless. Destiny always has a sad side to it. For instance, I, who was always longing to be free, have chained my life: I shall never be alone, never free. I shall be surrounded with the etiquette of a court, whose principal victim I shall be ...[1]

The melancholy fiancée wished to keep contact with the only one of her childhood friends who was *en poste* in Paris. A few

[1] *Lettres familières de l'Impératrice Eugénie,* Vol. I, p. 50–3.

days before her marriage, she wrote to the Count of Galve: "*Mi querido Enrique*—the Emperor is dining with us and has asked me to invite you. I hope you will come. There will be no one but himself, his *aide-de-camp*, Mama and myself. After dinner, you can leave if you are bored. Don't fail to come ..." [1]

Mérimée had not been wrong in thinking that there was a reconciliation between the Emperor and Miss Howard. There had been nine clear days between Saint-Sylvestre and the ball at the Palace. The irreproachable Eugénie having accepted from a monarch prodigal of his attentions only those due to purity, the Sovereign endowed his ardent and tender mistress with the balance of the currency of his passion. He placed to his mistress's credit a considerable sum in discharge of all his liabilities.

[1] *idem*, p. 51.

CHAPTER SEVEN

THE LOVE LETTERS

In January 1853 Miss Howard was gratified to receive a flattering mark of confidence. The Emperor told her that she was to go to London on a confidential mission. Having been associated in the past with the Pretender's early political manœuvres, she had acquired, in his shadow, a certain experience of affairs. A charming woman, armed with a British passport, might now render real service to the cause of the French Empire. Had she not remained on good terms with a number of influential Englishmen, who had been frequenters of her salon in the days when they played high and hunted the fox?

It was a matter of looking into an obscure and unpleasant affair in London, where the Emperor was threatened with scandal by a blackmailer ... If " his dear and faithful Harriet " agreed to go to England, their friend Jean Mocquard would be selected to accompany her upon the short journey.

She accepted because she hoped to find in this new and active role a remedy for her broken heart. To be the master's special envoy was in a sense to belong to him still. As, unmarried, she had played the part of a morganatic wife, so she would now be an ambassadress in His Majesty's service without letters of credence. Even the name of " secret agent " seemed to suggest mysterious excitements.

It was agreed that on the 22nd January, 1853, in the early morning, Harriet and Mocquard would start in her travelling carriage. The travellers would go straight to Le Havre to, embark for England. But, on the appointed day, an unforeseen storm altered their arrangements. Mocquard and " the young English lady " had to spend the night in an inn near the harbour. On the morning of the 23rd, Miss Howard, while awaiting the Southampton packet, sent for a newspaper, opened it, and read: " His Majesty the Emperor yesterday announced to a State gathering in the Throne-room at midday his engagement to Mlle de Montijo y Kirkpatrick, Comtesse de Teba . . ."

Why hadn't Napoleon told her the truth? She had admitted the necessity for a political marriage. When, later, he had fallen in love with the little Montijo, she had realised, before he did, that he would marry the girl . . . Had not King Jérôme said of his Imperial nephew: " Louis will marry, if she wishes it, the first woman who refuses him her favours! " ?

Miss Howard had even been ready to approve his surprising choice, if the Emperor's domestic happiness really demanded that Harriet should be sacrificed and Eugénie wear the Crown. But why had he sent his mistress away by a trick, why had he presented her with the accomplished fact? Undoubtedly because " the blinds of his soul were always lowered " and because " you would have had to break open the Emperor's head to know what was going on inside it."

Outraged, Miss Howard blamed Mocquard. She had her horses harnessed and curtly ordered her dumbfounded coachman to drive back to Paris with all speed. The breaking of an axle-tree, too opportune to be accidental, made them lose half a day in the wilds of the country. While a village wheelwright repaired the broken part with incredible slowness, Mocquard lectured the forsaken woman. She wept a lot and then calmed down.

The situation was now perfectly clear and Mocquard knew it better than anyone: Napoleon III, madly in love with his Eugénie, was going to have her crowned Empress. An honorary mistress was to slide out of his life. He wished to indemnify her, but did not want to be importuned. The Emperor had already made, verbally, concrete offers. Was the dismissed mistress in agreement with him upon the clauses of their contract of separation?

She replied that she wished to see the Emperor in order to resolve certain questions connected with this sentimental drama:

(1) Since His Majesty wished it, Miss Howard promised to marry, but she desired to have the right to choose her future husband for herself. To the " honourable match " proposed (a widower official who had now reached the age of retirement), she said that she preferred " no matter what Englishman."

(2) As she had never disturbed the peace, nor committed the least crime, she did not wish to be exiled two hundred miles from Paris. The Emperor should be content with relegating his victim in Seine-et-Oise! Since the month of September 1852, fearing the worst, she had been organising a refuge for herself. Fond of investing in real estate, she had bought there a property of 460 acres, 34 roods comprising the house and park of Beauregard (at a cost of five hundred and seventy-five thousand francs), the farm of Béchevêt (for five hundred and thirty thousand francs) and the stud farm at Bel-Ébat (for three hundred and forty-five thousand francs). If, in conformity with the practice of the ancient monarchy, Miss Howard was to be placed somewhere in forced residence, let it at least be upon her own property.

(3) If the lady of the manor was thereupon to be made Comtesse de Beauregard, what name would her son bear? She was concerned about the matter. In England, Scotland and Ireland certain titles can be transmitted through the female line. Did Mocquard know whether this was the case in France? In the interests of Martin, the future Comtesse insisted upon a hereditary title.

(4) She also wished to continue the guardianship of " her well-beloved adopted sons," Louis and Eugène, non-legitimised bastards of France.

The *chef de cabinet* took note of these requests and thought himself in a position to say that her wishes would be granted.

When Miss Howard got home, she found her house in curious disorder; her servants seemed to have disappeared. In the big yellow drawing-room with its stuffed sofas, the Boule furniture had been burst open and had disgorged a flood of music scores, herbals and albums, though not a picture was missing from the walls. Her valuable silver still shone in the showcases and the delicate old Vincennes china upon the shelves had not suffered.

Harriet ran up to the first floor where the contents of her well-supplied wardrobe had been thrown upon the floor and trampled on. Lace, furs and linen formed a frivolous heap upon the ground. Her women, coming at the sound of her cries, burst into tears, though they could not explain intelligently what had happened. They told the absurd stories which uneducated people are liable to invent when they have been seriously frightened.

Going into her boudoir, Miss Howard suddenly understood what had occurred. All the locks had been broken open. Her gaping desk, its secret drawer torn out, was like a reliquary sacrilegiously profaned. She found her jewels complete in their caskets lined with black velvet. Not a pendant nor an ear-ring was missing, but she no longer possessed a single letter from the Emperor Napoleon III.

Was it an indictable act? . . . A burglary? . . . It was no more than an authorised search. Maupas, the Prefect of Police, who had once been the pitiless analyst of the stir created by the radiant appearance of Miss Howard at the Tuileries on the night of the Court ball, had received the order to search the house of the young woman who had been sent to London.

As Eugenia at the ball, so Harriet now demanded an immediate audience from the offender, whatever he might be doing. "Napoleon III went to the Rue du Cirque. What passed between him and his mistress no one has ever known . . . In the

duel between the two lovers, the Emperor had begun by dis-
arming his adversary . . ." [1] The duel over, there was a reconciliation upon the field.

Harriet had demanded four amendments to the contract of
separation. Over and above them she obtained a fifth and
extraordinary concession:

(1) Miss Howard was authorised to marry an Englishman.
Her liberty of choice might extend to any British citizen whether
bachelor, widower or divorced.

(2) The ex-favourite would become Comtesse de Beauregard
and de Béchevêt, when these noble lands had been made a
majorat. And, as Agnès Sorel had been Dame de Beauté, so
Harriet Howard would become Dame de Bel-Ébat.

(3) Martin, her natural heir, was to succeed her in her privileges,
dignities and lands. Granting him French nationality, the
Emperor offered the young man a diplomatic career.

(4) Eugène and Louis would not be removed from her guardianship. During the whole of their schooling, the Vergeot
sons would share Martin's life, until they had chosen a profession
for themselves or developed a vocation. Alexandrine Vergeot,
their mother, was perfectly agreeable to the plan. She was the
more willing to agree to it since she now had a third child, born
on the 12th August, 1850, by her liaison with Pierre Bure,
treasurer-general to the Crown.

(5) Miss Howard had added to the Crown furniture in the
apartments at Saint-Cloud portraits, bronzes and china which
were her private property. Without having explicitly asked for
it, she received permission to stay in the Palace as the Emperor
thought that she would like to oversee the packing and moving
of her treasures and personal effects.

On Monday, 24th January, 1853, the Emperor drew up with
his own hand the draft of the letters patent by which Miss
Howard was to become Comtesse de Beauregard. It was not
yet the official document, but nevertheless a valuable paper for

[1] Léon Treich, *Les Alcôves de Napoléon III*, p. 61.

the pacification of an outraged woman. It was a useful thing to be able to send round to the Rue du Cirque.

In parentheses, it may be said here, that when, much later, Harriet wished to gather together the flotsam and jetsam of her past in order to compose what at that time was known as a " *Tombeau*," her patent of nobility was enshrined in a folio superbly bound by Rivière in full blue morocco.[1]

To Lord John Russell, much concerned about the Emperor's marriage, Lord Cowley sent some picturesque details:

" I found Drouyn de Lhuys much distressed at all that is going on here. He said he was very glad to see me, for he much wished to ask my advice as to the conduct he should pursue in the very difficult circumstances in which he found himself. He had, as far as the middle of November, been suspicious that the Emperor had some idea of marrying Mlle de Montijo, and that he had addressed him a letter on the subject, which he read to me, showing the folly and danger of such a course. In reply the Emperor thanked him for it, and assured him that he had no intention of doing anything of the kind. In a subsequent letter, however, the Emperor said that it seemed that the Minister had known His Majesty's mind better than himself, for he had decided to marry Mlle de Montijo. The question then, which Drouyn de Lhuys asked himself was, could he, entertaining the opinions he did on that subject, continue honourably to be the Emperor's Minister . . ."[2]

[1] On the 25th July, 1933, at Sotheby's a collection was sold. In the catalogue of the auction is to be found, described under Lot 1654, the documents collected by Miss Howard in memory of a broken liaison.

Included in the collection were the documents concerning the *Sale of the effects of Louis-Napoleon BONAPARTE, at Messrs. Christie, Manson and Woods, on the 21st May, 1849*, that is to say the period when the Pretender had left England to conquer his throne.

The single letter, which by a miracle escaped the search of the 22nd January, 1853, was piously preserved in this album: *Letter from him to his mistress, Elizabeth A. Haryett, A.l.s., 8 pages . . .*

Neither Mr. Ivor Guest, when he was writing his remarkable work *Napoleon III in England*, nor I last year, have succeeded in discovering where these Imperial relics are to-day. The House of Sotheby unhappily no longer know to whom these documents *all inlaid to folio size and bound in full blue morocco jansenist, inside dentelles*, were sold in 1933. I should have liked to acquire them, or at least examine them. Surely they must still be in existence in some collector's library. *Où sont les neiges d'antan?*

[2] *The Paris Embassy during the Second Empire*, the papers of Lord Cowley, edited by his son, p. 16.

Miss Howard, who was very meticulous about such things as paintings and *bibelots*, sadly packed her belongings on the ground floor of the Château of Saint-Cloud. She was still there on Sunday, 30th January, at the hour when all the bells of Paris and the firing of guns at the Invalides announced that Eugénie, Empress of the French, was on her way back from Notre-Dame in the Coronation Coach.

The Court learnt that day with stupefaction that the august couple's honeymoon was to be spent in the cold little lodge of Villeneuve-l'Étang. The secret reason for this decision, apparently so inexplicable, was only known to a small number of intimate friends. Prosper Mérimée severely censured the " audacity " with which Miss Howard had taken up residence at Saint-Cloud, " in order to prevent Napoleon and the Empress passing their marriage night there."

Lord Cowley to Lord John Russell: " We have married the Emperor ... He could not have liked his reception by the people, who, I understand, showed the utmost indifference at the whole pageant. I have been confined to the house for the last three days and could not attend the ceremonies. That in the Notre-Dame was, I am told, beautiful." [1]

The Comtesse de Montijo who, since the engagement, had been living with her daughter at the Élysée, went back there alone after the wedding, exhausted and famished. Paris already glowed with a thousand fireworks. She found the Palace deserted and almost without lights. No food had been prepared for the Emperor's mother-in-law and she had to invite herself to dine with a friend.

Prosper Mérimée to Doña Manuela: It's a terrible thing to have daughters and to marry them off! But what can you expect? Holy Writ says that a woman shall quit her parents to follow her husband. Now all your duties as a mother have been fulfilled and, indeed,

[1] *The Paris Embassy during the Second Empire*, the Papers of Lord Cowley, p. 17–18.

no one can say that you have not married your daughters extremely well . . .[1]

It is also a terrible thing to have a lover and to lose him. Proud Miss Howard was deeply wounded. From Saint-Cloud, she wrote the Emperor a letter which must have affected him, for he preserved it until the end of his reign. When, in 1870, this prophetic letter was found at the Tuileries, Napoleon III had been defeated, the Empress Regent was in exile and Harriet had been dead for five years . . . It is the only letter of hers to the Emperor which has been published. Why did he keep it? Perhaps as a memorial to the only woman who had ever really loved him.

Sire, I am leaving. I could easily have sacrificed myself to political necessity, but I cannot forgive you for sacrificing me for a whim. I am taking your children with me and, like another Josephine, your star.

I ask only for one last interview to say an eternal good-bye. I hope you will not refuse me . . .[2]

Miss Howard left Saint-Cloud and went to her own house in the Rue du Cirque in order to await events. She did not admit defeat. The Court and the town watched her every action.

Journal de Viel-Castel, 6th February, 1853: Mme Howard, the Emperor's ex-mistress, has not left Paris. She even makes a point of placing herself in their way, when he comes to Paris with the Empress, and of saluting them. The Emperor replies. Mme Howard believes that, once the honeymoon is over, the Emperor will come and see her on a friendly basis. I hope not, for one may be Mme Howard's lover, but one cannot be her friend.

[1] *Lettres de Prosper Mérimée à la Comtesse de Montijo*, published under the auspices of the Duke of Alba, Vol. I, p. 356.
[2] cf. M. Fravaton, *Le Château de Beauregard, an article* published in the *Revue de l'Histoire de Versailles*, 12th years, No. 1, pp. 41–2, in 1910.

It appears certain (according, it is true, to somewhat ill-disposed persons) that the Emperor gives her a pension of two hundred thousand francs. I am sure that this is a lie: one does not pay a discarded mistress as much as that! . . .

The Empress had asked for Mérimée as her secretary; the Emperor refused . . . Mérimée has been the lover of Mme de Montijo . . .[1]

And Arsène Houssaye, in his charming Oriental story, transforms the double drama of the incomplete break and the ill-fated marriage as follows:

There were always two camps at the Court: those who were on the side of the mistress and those who played their part in the novelist's comedy. The former did everything they could to see that the mistress won, while the latter did not allow themselves to be outdistanced in the steeplechase.

The Emperor had returned to his capital . . . Wherever he went, on foot or by carriage, to the theatre or to the Bois, the huntress appeared before him, but like Virgil's young girl who fled beneath the boughs. Letters were always going to and fro . . . I will not recount the whole history in all its detail. The huntress was as unattainable as Diana; she triumphed over every inducement. She had not the wherewithal to buy dresses, but she thought only of her wedding-gown at Pekin. Besides, beauty has all the dressmakers at its feet. The Emperor reached a crisis of passion . . .

The mistress fought till the last moment, but she was abandoned even by those who had provided ladies-in-waiting for her. The courtiers fell away like beads from a broken necklace; nothing remained to her but tears for her lost lover. Her tears were pearls for they fell from the heart. It was not however of these pearls that the capital of the Celestial Empire made an incomparable necklace for the future Empress.

The wedding-day arrived. The bells rang out; the huntress triumphed, but a sad presentiment was felt, like a shiver, in every heart. It was because this young woman, who had no consideration in the country, suddenly assumed the face of destiny in the Celestial Empire. She is beautiful and charming, but who can tell? Behind

[1] *Mémoires du comte Horace de Viel-Castel*, Vol. II, p. 162.

the single line upon her forehead, there is a pride which may commit the whole Orient to fire and blood . . .[1]

It was time to audit the account. With love and money as the stake, Louis Napoleon had squandered his mistress's fortune. Having won and married, he wished at last to pay the debts of love.

The estate of Beauregard, to which Miss Howard wished to retire, is that which, in 1950, the Comte de Bendern, Councillor of State of the Principality of Liechtenstein, its last proprietor, presented to the City of Paris. The château dates from the seventeenth century and is full of historical memories. It is there that Lulli and Quinault, those friendly collaborators, met to compose *Amadis* and *Armide*. Nicole du Val, widow of a Councillor to the King, offered them the hospitality of this place so propitious for work. It was she who built, in 1689, the chapel which was joined by a gallery to the right wing of the château while a theatre was built on the opposite side. Thus the guests could pass from divine service to drawing-room comedy without leaving the house.

Later, Louis XV came from Versailles to hunt with the Comte de Montaigu at Beauregard. Under the Empire, Mme de Boigne, famous diarist and generous hostess, invited Mme Récamier to stay there. One day, alas, the Comte de Boigne having expressed to his wife his " polite desire never to see her again," she had to leave her husband's house.

For the previous forty years (1812–52), four successive owners having decided to resell Beauregard at once, it had been left empty. To restore the decaying fabric, whose vast rooms had been left to " rats, moths and bookworms," Miss Howard was going to need considerable sums of money. Besides the pompous succession of reception rooms and the two dining-rooms, the new owner would have to furnish sixteen master bedrooms and twelve servants' rooms; do up the outbuildings: " stabling for

[1] Arsène Houssaye, *Les Trois Rayonnantes*, pp. 211-13.

sixteen horses, coach-houses for ten carriages, a cowhouse for sixteen cows, dairy and cheese house." To follow the fashion of the times, she also intended to create two " winter gardens," hot-houses for exotic plants where chairs and settees would stand beneath the palms and flowering camellias.

The Emperor determined that Miss Howard should be completely refunded for the advances she had made during the first conspiracy and the further huge loans at the time of the *coup d'état*. He had taken back his love letters; she would be paid their weight in bank notes!

A first instalment was paid on the 25th March, 1853. The ex-mistress gave her receipt under her private sign manual:

I affirm, by these presents, that I have received from His Majesty the Emperor Napoleon III the sum of one million francs, in complete acquittal and discharge of all my rights and interests in the estate of Civita-Nova on the borders of Ancona in the Papal States. *81338*

Paris, 25th *March*, 1853.   E. H. DE BEAUREGARD [1]

E. H. de Beauregard stood for Elizabeth Haryett de Beauregard for, on the eve of starting a new life, the lady of the manor had resumed her old Christian name. An amusing letter, written to one of her adopted sons, is signed Old Mother Bess. Miss Melliora Findon, her pretended younger sister, called her Lizzie.

As for the surname, in order to purchase Beauregard, Béchevêt and Bel-Ébat, she had had according to custom to appear before Maître Roquebert, lawyer to the Baron de Guenifey, the vendor, and draw up various documents. Here she assumed British nationality and a false identity. She called herself Mrs. Elizabeth Alderton, widow of the late Martin Haryett, landowner, domiciled at 9 Berkeley Street, London, at present living in Paris at

---

[1] *Papiers et Correspondance de la famille impériale*, Vol. I, p. 171. (Paris, Imprimerie Nationale, 1870.)

14 Rue du Cirque.[1] A slightly different imposture to that which had covered Martin's birth with fictitious legitimacy. To him, she had given her own parents, but a similar substitution would now have made Mrs. Joseph Gawen Haryett, née Alderton, the veritable proprietor of the estates acquired by her daughter! This was the reason for the variant and the invention of the false husband: Martin Haryett, senior.

As she was paying immediate cash down, Maître Roquebert did not ask her to establish her identity, nor did he demand her marriage lines, or her husband's death certificate.

To give credence to the lie, Miss Howard told several people in Versailles a plausible and touching story of her being married to an officer in the Indian Army who was " soon killed in action." The death of the hero was supposed to have preceded the birth of the posthumous orphan. The misfortune of a young mother, left alone in the world at the age of twenty, having moved many of her auditors, she soon added to it an equally imaginative prologue: her recollections of her English childhood. In this unwritten autobiography, constantly repeated and elaborated, the innocent Elizabeth had not been an actress who had left the stage to become a courtesan, but a church-going Protestant, living a life of retired gentility. But the figure of the imaginary husband was, a few months later, to take on extraordinary life.

She said of Napoleon III that, soon after he had escaped from the Fortress of Ham, he had confided to her the delicate and dangerous honour of educating his two sons. Once the Empire had been re-established, Mme Howard would merely, like Mme de Maintenon, have been named Governess to the bastard children of France. As painted by herself, that particular Howard was a young woman of irreproachable character who was most unjustly calumniated.

At Marly, as at Bougival, the myth of her widowhood was

[1] The Archives of Maître Jacques Mahot de la Quérantonnais, great-grandson and direct successor of Maître Amédée Mocquard, the Imperial lawyer.

believed but, in other parts of France, the proposed raising of the estate of Beauregard to a territorial title aroused a good deal of anger. The Costa de Beauregards, the Labrousse de Beauregards, the Savary de Beauregards, the Turquet de Beauregards, the Sourdeau de Beauregards, and a diversity of Beauregards without the particle would not tolerate that the Emperor should give their name, honourable and respected as it was, to " a loose-living foreigner "! They were resolved to seek justice in the courts, if ever the Imperial act legalised this revolting homonym.

The Emperor, extremely put out, surrendered to the legitimate objections put forward by the Beauregards by divine right. He decided to postpone and temporise. The strength of his inertia was formidable.

If Miss Howard had been content with the title of Béchevêt, she could have had this available name without further difficulty. But from feminine caprice, the siren with the long eyelashes attached a symbolic and musical value to the word Beauregard. She took it literally as homage rendered to the beauty of her eyes: " Beauregard suits me, Beauregard sounds just like me. I shall be Lady Fairlook or no lady at all! " she wrote with arch obstinacy ... Deprived, through her own fault, of the decree which would have confirmed her pretensions, she merely assumed what she was refused and became Comtesse de Beauregard as she had been Miss Howard, without patents or parchments. The Emperor let her do as she would. The Commissioner at the Sceau de France closed his eyes to it. Harriet thought that in showing a bold front to the Beauregards, she would become a comtesse by the mere possession of the estate. Things remained in suspense. Harriet, who had become Elizabeth Ann again, awaited the proper moment. Then she completely forgot her curious heraldic position.

The problem was finally resolved in the following way. Ten years after the Emperor's marriage, Martin Constantine Haryett, son of the supposed comtesse called of Beauregard and now of age, discovered the truth. Angrily desirous of obtaining, both for himself and his descendants, a proper right to the title, he decided to take steps. By an Imperial decree, dated the 9th January, 1864, Napoleon III gave him his patent of nobility.

Harriet, then on her death bed, was not included in the document.

CHAPTER EIGHT

THE LIFE OF AN EMPRESS

PALACE LIFE is not propitious to married happiness and a honeymoon atmosphere is soon corrupted by it. Husband and wife cannot find in it a climate suited to the difficult adjustments of people who, before marriage, know each other but little. Having each their own civil and military establishments, their time subject to an inflexible programme imposed by State duties, often attending ceremonies separately, how can they devote themselves to each other? They can never have a meal alone because their suites eat with them. If they wish to please a public curious about their every action, they must show themselves, bow and smile to the crowd. They are condemned to live in public.

Between the beautiful Empress and her greying Emperor, there was incompatibility of age, attitude and temperament. Eugénie, daughter of a *camarera mayor*, had lived much at the Court of Spain where the strictest etiquette ruled, not only over the speech of courtiers, but over that of royal personages themselves. When Napoleon III addressed her in public in the familiar second person singular, calling her his *Ugénie*, she was startled; when, speaking of her in her presence to a third party, he said " my wife " instead of " the Empress," her expression showed displeasure.

A first disagreement had come between the august couple a few days after the wedding celebrations. Eugénie had her family at heart. She wanted her sister to have a splendid Hôtel d'Alba upon the Champs Élysées. In the month of January 1853 the Emperor had lodged his fiancée and Doña Manuela at the Élysée, and they had both imagined that the vacant Palace would be the permanent residence of Madame Belle-Mère. The latter was, on the contrary, "discreetly invited" at the beginning of March to cross the frontier. The reason for the old comtesse's expulsion was her tiresome habit of never paying her tradesmen. As they became more pressing, they had begun to present themselves at the Tuileries to demand their due from the Civil List! And the exasperated Emperor considered himself morally bound to pay.

Also, at about this time, the Emperor learnt that Mme de Montijo had had numerous affairs in many countries. Prosper Mérimée, once her episodic lover but now promoted to permanent confidant, seemed to be hand in glove with the embarrassing dowager. When the Empress's household was being formed and Eugénie wanted Mérimée as her controlling secretary, the Emperor decisively refused. Doña Manuela left Paris on the 19th March without the Sovereigns seeing her off at the station. She left in a fury. Mérimée accompanied her as far as Poitiers. She was never again asked to stay at the Tuileries. Napoleon III could not banish her from the country nor prevent her coming on visits but, when in Paris, she always stayed at a hotel.

At the Palace, their marriage nights were not of the happiest. The essential duty of a sovereign's wife being to produce an heir, Eugénie submitted to her conjugal duties. But she never enjoyed them. The passion of physical love shocked her to the point that she one day said to a friend, who was too indiscreet not to repeat it, "But, really, why do men never think of anything but *that*?" On his side the Emperor had doubtless not realised that there were women who were totally unresponsive. His wife's coldness disappointed him. He regretted his " dear and faithful Harriet."

The Minister of Police set a watch upon the inconsolable

woman who, having retired to Versailles, directed from there the great building operations proceeding at Beauregard. The château, given over to restoring workmen, was uninhabitable.

Maupas had appointed as his personal spy an impoverished man of fashion at a salary, very large for the period, of a thousand gold francs a month. The elegant informer communicated directly with his chief and sent him a report every day in the form of a lively, unsigned letter.

28th March, 1853: Miss Howard is the subject of much talk . . . She is going to be given a peerage with the title of Princess. The noble lady is still living at Versailles. She is often to be met with walking by the lake, like the goddess Calypso after the departure of Ulysses! A woman, who saw her the other day, said maliciously that "her position is interesting." Miss Howard has not, like Calypso, nymphs who endeavour to console her by making music for her, but she possesses a tom-cat, angora by race, which breaks the china and wears a *green* ribbon on its tail. This lucky cat has its own servant, so it is said in the Faubourg Saint-Germain (who are taking greater and greater interest in the intimate details of the Emperor's life); the servant wears a *green livery*. The cat and its servant are gauges of affection from the absent one. Moreover, Miss Howard is not altogether without *hopes* concerning the latter. She uses an expression which we repeat without comprehension: "He has always had whims," she says, "but he is subject to pains in his stomach, and I very well know that he will come back to me!"

1st April, 1853: People are still talking about Miss Howard. At the moment they're marrying her off to an Englishman. She will be given a large marriage portion by the Emperor . . .

Society is still very sorry for Her Majesty the Empress's lot. Profound boredom has been succeeded by violent chagrin. Accustomed to being free, she is a prisoner; from being Queen of Fashion, she has become the slave of etiquette! As soon as she was married, the Emperor separated her from her mother . . . Everyone has noticed her expression of dejection and despondency at the recent balls . . .

5th April, 1853: I am still told that the Empress is very bored . . .

The Emperor does not wish her to go out alone. A few days ago, when he was extremely busy, the Empress wanted to order a carriage and go out with a lady-in-waiting. The Emperor was warned in time . . . She was ordered to remain at home . . .[1]

All the above is confirmed by the intimate and confidential correspondence between Eugénie and her distant sister:

The Empress Eugénie to the Duchess of Alba, 6th April, 1853: For God's sake write to me . . . It would only be charitable to do so. Tell James too. You see what long letters I write you . . . I think of you when they bring me gowns to choose from, for I have so many that, like children who have eaten too much jam, I am disgusted by them . . . From seeing so many lovely things, I choose the ugliest . . . Even *caged* as I am, I can do your commissions for you.

What I shall miss this summer is not being able to drive with you without being recognised: I fear I shall not be *allowed* to . . . Tell me what has happened to the fans; I would like to know if I must give up hope of receiving them . . . When I think of *our salon*, where you all gathered every night, I feel very sad, for God knows whether I shall ever be able to take my place in it again and, if I can, in what circumstances it may be? But I have made a rule not to want what I cannot get . . .[2]

Guizot, the wise and Protestant Guizot, kept Mme de Gasparin in touch with the post-marriage news: "It is said that the Imperial marriage still goes well. The Emperor, however, has boils and has not been out for several days. He has had to have a slight operation. It is said that ' the Emperor has boiled away . . .' Some say that the Empress is bored; others say that she enjoys herself very much, attending her husband's bedside . . ."[3]

On the 29th April, 1853, after a very hot bath, the Empress

---

[1] Archives of the Imperial Ministry of Police, quoted by Charles Nauroy in *Les Secrets des Bonaparte,* pp. 76–9.

[2] *Lettres familières de l'impératrice Eugénie,* Vol. 1, pp. 67–9.

[3] cf. André Gayot, *François Guizot et Madame Laure de Gasparin,* p. 394.

had a serious hæmorrhage. The doctors immediately diagnosed
"the result of a pregnancy" which, according to them, "dated
from approximately two months back." The official *Moniteur*
informed the public of the mishap. The immodest communiqué
gave cause for scandal, for the tradition of European courts was
that an Imperial or Royal pregnancy was only officially recognised when the pregnant Sovereign had reached the fourth
month. The irascible Viel-Castel thundered:

> The Empress has had a miscarriage ... Her pregnancy was not
> far advanced. The Grand Masters of Ceremonies have thought it
> right to announce the miscarriage in the *Moniteur*, whereas her
> pregnancy had not even been announced! Where can these gentle-
> men have learnt their manners? ... Day by day, we were told
> the minutest details of the Empress's state of health; it was talked
> about in the most indecent way! This is only what one may
> expect from the gilded pimps of the Tuileries.
>
> Mocquard, *chef de cabinet* to the Emperor, allows himself to be
> seen in a box at the opera with Mme Howard, who has been given
> a huge fortune as well as a château near Versailles. This woman
> still has considerable influence and I fear that she may be restored
> to her previous position ...[1]

In more measured terms, the wise Guizot expressed a similar
opinion to the choleric Viel-Castel:

> The miscarriage has happened. We have been expecting it for
> the last eight days. Would she make the grade or would she not?
> I have heard very knowledgeable discussions about the matter from
> a number of beautiful women: "Is she pregnant? Or is she not?
> How long gone is she? What does her husband say? What does
> the doctor say?" We have been hearing about it for some time.
> I have always admired the pleasure with which women talk openly
> about these indecent matters. ...[2]

Lord Clarendon, who had succeeded Lord John Russell at the

[1] *Mémoires du comte Horace de Viel-Castel*, Vol. II, p. 183.
[2] Letter quoted by André Gayot in *François Guizot et Madame Laure de Gasparin*, p. 395.

Foreign Office, was no less interested than these happy gossips in gynæcological matters. Cowley, the Ambassador, had written to him: "The Emperor, on my condoling with him, said: 'C'est faute à réparer.'" The British Foreign Secretary replied: "An affair of that kind is not always as *facile à réparer* as His Majesty seems to think."

> *Lord Cowley to Lord Clarendon*, 1st May, 1853: "I am very much inclined to think, from various circumstances that have come to my knowledge, that the Empress has never been in an interesting situation at all. That it was a false alarm but that the Court was ashamed to own that it was a flash in the pan; and they therefore thought that it was better to make the world believe, through the columns of the *Moniteur*, that there had been something. This is truly French. On the other hand, the *Faubourg* swears that the child dates from October at Fontainebleau and that the *fausse couche* has been brought about to save Her Majesty's reputation."

> Lord Clarendon commented: "How very French the whole history of the Empress's beginning, continuation and end of parturiency has been. I doubt her having children." [1]

Elizabeth Haryett, Comtesse de Beauregard, announced the news to an English friend in these terms: "The Court circular gives information that Her Majesty gloriously miscarried. Nobody knew she was in the family way, not even her gracious self. Anyhow, the mamaship is a failure..." [2] In the ex-mistress's correspondence the legitimate wife held an exaggerated place.

We know, since the publication of the *Lettres familières* of the Empress Eugénie by her great-nephew, the seventeenth Duke of Alba, that there was in fact a pregnancy and an accidental miscarriage in 1853. The person most interested bears witness to it in her correspondence with her elder sister:

> *The Empress Eugénie to the Duchess of Alba*, 1st May, 1853: I have

---

[1] *The Paris Embassy during the Second Empire*, Lord Cowley's papers, pp. 19-20.
[2] Unpublished letter. Private collection.

now been lying in bed for a fortnight without moving, and God knows how much longer I shall have to do so? I was very ill for seventeen hours. The pains gave me cold sweats. Indeed, M. Dubois told me that I now know what it is to be confined . . . I regret having suffered so much in vain. I was so happy at the thought of having a pretty baby like yours,[1] and I was in despair . . . Perhaps it will be all the better for my health not to get well too quickly. All the same, I must admit, that I am already impatient at having to stay in bed . . .

3rd May, 1853: I can see, from your letter, that you had not yet heard what had happened, since you give me every encouragement to bear my suffering! What is so sad, is to think that it has all been useless. I suppose it had to happen! . . . I go mad with joy when I think that I shall soon be able to hold you in my arms. The mere idea of it makes me forget the boredom of the days I must spend in my room, with the prospect of remaining there throughout the month of May, but, since I dream of nothing but June, it is all bearable. For the love of God, don't forget how much I want to see you, and that it would be sheer cruelty to put off your journey . . . I have been so ill that to think of you as pregnant frightens me . . . When I say that I do not like children, I think it must be from jealousy . . . To have one like yours, I would give my right arm . . .

How delighted I am that the hats pleased you! I have similar ones, but have not yet worn them as I am confined to bed. I have ordered a mantle for you. Tell me, shall I keep it till you come? I think I had better send it to you, because I remember the celebrated green mantle which made us laugh so much when you were pregnant for the first time. Do you remember it? . . .

8th May, 1853: Your letter No. 7 gave me great pleasure . . . I, too, often think of the past and remember all that I have given up for ever: the house at Aranjuez where we were together; and Romanillos which, even at Fontainebleau or at Compiègne, I can never forget. You remind me of a thousand things which made those places, which I shall never see again, so delightful! In exchange for them, I have gained a crown, but what does that signify? . . . I am the first slave of my kingdom; isolated in a crown;

[1] The Duchess of Alba, who was pregnant, was to give birth on the 19th October to her daughter, Maria-Louisa (1853-76), future Duchess of Medinacelli, who died in childbirth at the age of twenty-three.

without a woman friend and, it goes without saying, without a man friend either; never alone for a moment; an insufferable existence . . .

Dear Sister, I thank God that I have not realised the hope which filled me with such joy, for I think fearfully of the poor Dauphin, Louis XVII . . . Who knows what might have been the sad fate of my child! . . . You can see from this that my thoughts are not happy ones, but you must realise that to-day, I have been in bed for twenty-two days . . . I am beginning to become extremely depressed . . . To-day, I wanted to try to stand, but I could not, so great is my weakness, the result doubtless of loss of blood . . . Mamma believes that it would not have happened had she been here. As if that were possible! You can imagine how well I have been looked after . . . Don't remove my bed from your room at Romanillos; for by that you will think of me . . .[1]

A Spaniard, called Pedro Gil, who had opened a bank in Paris at 23 Rue Saint-Georges, was commissioned by Mocquard, (1) to pay all the Montijo debts; and (2) to indemnify Miss Howard by successive payments of fifty thousand francs. This confidential agent was more or less promoted to the position of financial adviser to the Privy Purse.

The Court was in a state of excitement. It was known that, upon the national holiday of the 15th August, a number of civilians were to be decorated with the Legion of Honour. The Empress put forward her candidate for the cross: Horace de Viel-Castel. Jean Mocquard, who was already *Chevalier*, was intriguing for the rosette. Achille Fould, the Minister, was studying the citations. Viel-Castel, fearful and suspicious, noted in his *Journal*:

11*th August*, 1853: Will the Emperor remember the spontaneous promise he was kind enough to make me on the 14th March last? Will the Empress remember that she said to me: " I won't let him forget his promise to you "? . . .

14*th August*, 1853: Three days ago, after luncheon, the Empress said to the Emperor:

[1] *Lettres familières de l'Impératrice Eugénie*, Vol. I, pp. 76–86.

" Louis, we promised the Cross to M. de Viel-Castel: try not to forget it! "

The Emperor replied:

" We shall see."

The Empress was not at all satisfied with this answer.

" It is not ' we shall see ' that I wish to hear! You promised; and you must keep it."

What I say to myself is: " We shall see to-morrow."

15th August, 1853: In the *Moniteur* of this morning, there are four appointments of *Officiers* and *Chevaliers*:

Officiers
> Mocquard, Secretary to the Emperor.
> Conneau, Principal Physician.

Chevaliers
> Ch. Thélin, Keeper of the Privy Purse.
> Acar, Principal Pharmacist.

Conneau is a devoted friend; Thélin is, I believe, a foster-brother; I have no objections to these. But Acar, the Pharmacist! And Mocquard, is it because he served as the Emperor's white eunuch to Mme Howard? Is it because he cheapened his wife and daughter by taking them to a box at the opera with Mme Howard? . . . Poor Legion of Honour! . . .

16th August, 1853: I am fifty-one to-day. Yesterday, the Emperor should have given me the Cross. He had promised it to me, but has failed to keep his promise. Fould was opposed to it . . .[1]

Mocquard was not afraid of appearing in public with the Comtesse de Beauregard because the latter had at this time regained favour with Napoléon III. The Emperor was seeing her again. Like all weak and unstable characters, he would go back on his tracks in his love affairs, sometimes from remorse.

Whenever Napoléon III went to inspect his troops in the camp at Satory, the favourite, driving herself in a light open carriage, was to be met with on the road. From a house at Loges, Mme Brinquant watched her Sovereign playing truant.

[1] *Mémoires du comte Horace de Viel-Castel*, Vol. II, pp. 219–26.

III

In her old age she evoked her memories of the Second Empire for Marcel Fouquier. The drawings of Constantin Guys reminded her, she said, of Miss Howard and her smart turn-out. In his *Jours heureux d'autrefois*, Fouquier has noted:

> I sometimes used to go out to the Brinquants at Loges in the neighbourhood of Versailles. I cannot forget a story which was told me by the elder Mme Brinquant and which has all the atmosphere of its period. Napoleon III had come to Versailles in order to review the troops in the camp of Satory ... After the march past, he re-entered a carriage that was waiting for him. It was Miss Howard's ... with whom he used to go to the Château de Beauregard, next door to Chesnay. In order to exchange his uniform for plain clothes, he used, in the carriage, to take off his military cap and his tunic and put on a top hat and frock coat, retaining his red uniform trousers and his polished boots. Those who saw him going through the streets of Versailles in this peculiar attire in Miss Howard's pony-chaise have never forgotten it. His love for the beautiful Englishwoman explained everything ...[1]

The Empress, unsatisfied, disliked the physical act of love to such an extent that she referred to it in her private conversations with her ladies-in-waiting as *disgusting*. But when the ladies thought it their duty to inform her privately that the Emperor had returned to his mistress, there were tears and gnashings of teeth at the château.

From the time of this first infidelity—and her husband was too sensual not to be fickle—Eugénie brought into play a defence which, for three successive years, in similar case, enabled her to regain the advantage. She decreed a suspension of all legitimate relations and forbade her lord and master access to her room. But Napoleon III desired by his marriage a son who would be eligible to wear the crown forbidden the Vergeot bastards. The Empress, legally married, could alone of all women give him a Prince Imperial. The " dear and faithful Harriet " was fatally out of the running, though the breach only took place

[1] Marcel Fouquier, *Jours heureux d'autrefois*, pp. 15-16.

over a long period and with constant renewals of their relationship.

Maupas took a great interest in the changes of relationship
among the three people concerned. It was one of the subjects
of inquiry reserved for his personal informer, whose worldly
letters made the point:

2nd July, 1853: It is said that Louis Napoleon has completely
resumed his relations with Miss Howard, which has somewhat
clouded the Imperial marriage.

22nd September, 1853: The Empress, having learnt that there was
a reconciliation between the Emperor and Miss Howard (according
to some) or merely a correspondence (according to others), has
told her august husband that she intends leaving both Saint-Cloud
and France, if the Emperor has no greater regard for his dignity
and does not better realise the duty that he owes to the wife of his
choice. Something of a scene took place ... Her Majesty the
Empress told the Emperor that she did not care for the throne, but
only for her husband; that she had not married the Sovereign, but
the man; and that the first wrong he committed towards her would
be decisive ... The Emperor, always calm and gentle, even when
he is in the wrong, ultimately succeeded in calming her anger by
promising to break off all contact with the person in question.

21st September, 1853: Miss Howard is in the ascendant to the
Empress's great displeasure. The ex-mistress has expensive tastes ...
Quite recently he had to agree to giving her a hundred and fifty
thousand francs which M. Mocquard thought were essential in
order to keep her quiet ...[1]

It was a double policy of appeasement, for Napoleon III had
not only to pacify his mistress but manage his furious Empress.
Miss Howard received an order not to appear again in Paris and
was advised to make a long sojourn abroad. Not without regret,
the Emperor asked his friend to write to him no more; if she
had some important communication to make, Mocquard was
always there to transmit a " verbal message."

[1] Archives of the Imperial Minister of Police, quoted by Charles Nauroy in *Les Secrets
des Bonaparte*, pp. 119, 125, 127.

Harriet sadly gave way. In order to fulfil an essential clause of the treaty of 1852, she still had to find a husband. She went to London with Martin, Louis and Eugène. The three boys were delighted to visit England. " Old Mother Bess " hoped to enter them for some aristocratic school. But it was not everyone who could enter those imposing schools which had remained completely feudal.

In her own country Harriet met many old friends. A young woman worth five million gold francs (a million pounds of our money) never lacks for admirers and suitors. She reported that notorious libertines and hardened bachelors both proposed to her, and for good reason.

Her friends, the Normanbys, were still *en poste* in Florence, and they invited her to pay them a visit. Before accepting, she wrote to Mocquard, asking whether His Majesty would graciously authorise her to travel across France? Her magical château was then in full process of reconstruction; it was natural that the owner should wish to inspect the work in progress. The reply was a cordial permission to stay at Beauregard and even at 14 Rue du Cirque. The Emperor even condescended to encourage the journey to Italy. Was there a marriage on the stocks? Miss Howard was free to marry a Welsh baronet, a Roman count or a Wallachian lord provided she married someone. There is no country in which a handsome husband is not indispensable if beauty is to meet with respect. If, some day, Miss Howard brought a husband of good family back to Paris, she would be treated there as a " foreigner of quality," perhaps even received at Court . . .

In January 1854 the little house next door to the Élysée, which had long been sleeping behind its closed shutters, took on a festive air. Maupas's indefatigable correspondent reported:

7th February, 1854: The Empress is very sorrowful which people attribute either to her sadness at not having a child or to the unhappiness inflicted on her by her husband. There is much talk of a Mlle A. who appears to be, at the moment, the rival favoured by the Emperor. The old affection, now degenerated into friendship, for Miss Howard nevertheless continues and there are frequent visits to the Champs Élysées . . .

28th May, 1854: People are talking, as if it were an accomplished fact, of Miss Howard's marriage with " Sir Trelawny," a gentleman of the County of Cornwall. . . .[1]

[1] The Archives of the Imperial Minister of Police, quoted by Charles Nauroy in Les Secrets des Bonaparte, pp. 133-4.

CHAPTER NINE

RESIGNED TO MARRIAGE

THE NEWS was true. On the 16th May, 1854, in London, "Elizabeth Ann Haryett, spinster," had married a young man of good family called Clarence Trelawny.

The rugged lords of Trelawny Castle were his ancestors. Since the young man was the scion of an almost legendary race, he owed an epic and fabulous prestige to the Cornish ballads:

> And shall Trelawny die
> Here's twenty thousand Cornishmen
> Will know the reason why . . .

The Trelawny genealogy is to be found in Debrett. It is also authenticated by Burke.

A contemporary author, Mr. W. H. Holden, has published in a book of studies on nineteenth-century England[1]: *The Tragedy of Clarence Trelawny.*

"The Trelawnys of Trelawny are a Cornish family of great antiquity and distinction. According to Burke, they are descended from Eluni, Lord of Treloen in the reign of Edward the Confessor, and the first baronet was so created on the 1st July, 1628. In 1752 Lieutenant-General Harry Trelawny, younger brother of the sixth Baronet married Miss Mary Dormer, and early in Queen Victoria's reign we find their son, Captain Harry Brereton Trelawny, who had been an officer in the Grenadier Guards, settled at Shotwick Park in the County of Chester. Clarence, the third son of Captain

[1] W. H. Holden, *They Startled Grandfather.* (London, British Technical and General Press, 1950.)

Trelawny of Shotwick, was born on the 20th December, 1826, and although a younger son, his future should have been happy and prosperous. Yet his life was curiously unfortunate and, as we shall see, his death was sudden and tragic in the extreme . . .

"For some unexplained reason, he was not sent to one of our great Public Schools. Instead, he went to a most unsatisfactory school in France, where the conditions were brutally harsh; and often the unfortunate lad was so hungry, that he would collect orange peel and similar refuse from the gutters, which he gnawed to allay his continual hunger . . . Such a hard upbringing did little to ingrain in his character a proper respect for his parents or society in general. What is certain is that he grew up to become an outstandingly handsome young man, and that he obtained a commission in the Radetzky Hussars, a famous and aristocratic regiment in the Austrian Army. In the very striking uniform worn by his regiment, young Trelawny looked even more handsome than usual, and he turned the heads of many young ladies in the social set in which his brother officers moved; while it is equally certain that his own head became somewhat swollen in the process. Trelawny must have had many opportunities of contracting a brilliant marriage.

"His eldest brother, a Grenadier officer, died when Clarence was twenty-five years old; whereupon, another brother, who had married Lord Ormathwaite's daughter, became the heir to Shotwick, and Clarence himself became the second son . . ." [1]

To be the *second* son of a great landed proprietor, in a country where primogeniture has the force of law is not, in fact, a very great advantage. Clarence, a fashionable and prodigal officer, needed a good deal of money and ran into debt.

Mr. Ivor Guest, the author of *Napoleon III in England* tells us that Miss Howard married Clarence Trelawny, "a young Englishman of twenty-six serving in the Austrian Army, whom she had met lying ill in a French provincial hotel." [2] She herself told quite a different story: "We met in Florence; our mutual

[1] W. H. Holden, *The Tragedy of Clarence Trelawny*, chap. III of *They Startled Grandfather*, pp. 51–2.
[2] Ivor Guest, *Napoleon III in England*. (London, British Technical and General Press, p. 99.)

friend Lord Normanby introduced him to me, at the British Legation . . ." [1] What appears certain, is that the impoverished officer saw a desirable match in Mme de Beauregard. It mattered not in the least to him that she was three years older than himself and had a bastard child. Was she not unattached, extremely beautiful and divinely rich?

A few days after their meeting, he proposed that she should become his legitimate wife and as, at that precise moment, Miss Howard was seeking a marriageable Englishman, the matter was soon concluded. The terms of the contract were discussed. Out of loyalty to the memory of the Emperor, Harriet wished this completely legal marriage to be purely technical. For his part, Trelawny asked for certain financially profitable clauses to be inserted in the matrimonial contract. Against the pretensions of so greedy a fiancé, the devoted Strode defended as best he could the interests of a young mother whose fortune he administered with the thought constantly before him of her young son's future. Trelawny nevertheless obtained substantial advantages. The day before the marriage (15th May, 1854), a deed issued by William Mark Fladgate, solicitor, and superbly engrossed on parchment, made over to him the revenue in rents from the property his future wife possessed in London (houses in Mark Lane; the freehold of Nags Head Court, Gracechurch St.) and, from the funds administered by the trustees, an income for life of five hundred pounds sterling.

Martin Haryett, who was " mentioned and described " in the marriage settlement, does not appear there as the natural son of the bride. Even though there is no reference to his origins, the child of eleven was designated as the heir to Beauregard in France.

When, with a chivalrous gesture, a gallant man marries an unmarried mother, he normally legitimises the child from the past. Martin was not recognised by Trelawny. Too proud and sensitive to insist, Miss Howard did not try to persuade him to

[1] Unpublished letter in a private collection.

take the step, but she was much hurt. This was the first conjugal grievance.

The witnesses who, on the official forms, appended their signatures and seals at the bottom of the marriage contract were Nathaniel William John Strode, gentleman; Edward Moira, painter; and, naturally, Jean-Constant Mocquard. All three were present the following day at the religious ceremony in the church of St. James's, Piccadilly.[1] It was a sorry ceremony. The bride wept over her lost lover; Trelawny regretted having contracted a marriage which could be considered degrading. They hardly knew each other and did not look upon each other with any particular favour.

Clarence had not informed his relations of his intentions. An ironical notice, published in a London paper, informed their friends and acquaintances who had not been previously warned. The announcement in the *Gentleman's Magazine* " horrified his parents " when they discovered that the bride was " a successful courtesan . . . a notorious cast-off mistress of the Emperor of the French." Captain and Mrs. Trelawny steadfastly refused to receive their daughter-in-law. She was surprised and indignant. " She confidently expected that her marriage to Mr. Trelawny would assure her reception in English society. In these hopes she was bitterly disappointed," Holden wrote. The indifference of a clubman, who was content to pass his evenings among men at his club, and the shameful way in which her husband accepted invitations to fashionable dinner-parties from which she was excluded, added further grievances.

Having very little taste for soldiering, Trelawny sent in his papers. Paris tempted him. He persuaded Mrs. Trelawny, Comtesse de Beauregard in France, rashly to return there with him. They jointly bought a site, 154 Champs Elysées, of about two thousand square yards. Their property was bounded in the

---

[1] Hector Fleischmann, Adrien Dansette, Léon Treich, etc., all say that the marriage took place in Florence. Mr. Ivor Guest was the first to establish that it took place in the church of St. James's in London. We are in possession of a copy of the marriage lines.

east by the Rue Bel-Respiro, nowadays the Rue Arsène-Houssaye, on the north by the Boulevard Beaujon, now the Avenue Friedland, and on the west by the Rue Circulaire, later to become the Rue de Tilsitt.[1] They proposed building a town residence on the site. But, Trelawny House was never constructed. They lived at Beauregard and, for a few months during the summer, in Scotland. Clarence, a good shot, leased a shooting-box near Brahan in Ross-shire, grouse shooting being one of his favourite sports.

Above all a sportsman, he had married Beauregard, and especially Bel-Ébat, in order to have the enjoyment of a stud-farm. In a marriage he considered " degrading," the improvement of blood-stock became his principal object in life. As for Miss Howard, honorary favourite as she was, she had only added a husband to her household out of obedience to her Imperial lover.

An unhappy moon or, as Byron says, " a treacle moon " hung over them. The newly married couple felt nothing but contempt for each other. Two galley-slaves, chained together, they tried the strength of their fetters.

Elizabeth and Clarence Trelawny stayed, two years running, in the house they had leased four miles from Brahan.

" Why Scotland? " wrote the young wife. " Why? Because I am fond of lakes and tartans; chiefly because my husband is a fierce grouse killer."

At that time, Mary Stewart Mackenzie, the future Lady St. Helier, was growing up in a Highland castle. In her *Memories of Fifty Years*, published in 1909,[2] she recalls the arrival of the new tenants. No one in Ross-shire knew them. Nothing was known of them, except that Mrs. Trelawny was " though past her first youth, a very beautiful woman and magnificently

---

[1] From the Archives of Amédée Mocquard's chambers, placed at my disposal by Maître Mahot de La Quérantonnais.
[2] Lady St. Helier, *Memories of Fifty Years*. (London, Edward Arnold, 1909.)

dressed; her husband, a keen sportsman." To the general surprise, they did not make the usual social calls which were a ritual
in such circumstances. The whole county wondered at the
reasons for such bad manners.

Extremely curious, as little girls are, Mary Stewart Mackenzie
used to go and play on the road in order to watch the enigmatic
neighbour of whom the grown-ups spoke in low voices pass by,
either on horseback or in a carriage. All her life she was to
remember the abundant hair and the classic, forlorn profile.
So much beauty left an ineffaceable image in the fresh memory
of a young and attentive observer. The rigours of the Scotch
climate were detrimental to Clarence Trelawny's health. When
he fell ill and sent for a doctor, his wife's identity was revealed.
"The religious and moral sentiment of Ross-shire was so strong
that there was great difficulty in getting the doctor to continue
his attendance ... Even the tradespeople began to doubt
whether they were justified in supplying anybody with so stormy
a past ..."[1] Lady St. Helier concluded by saying that the tenant
of the lodge " disappeared as mysteriously as she came." After
such incidents, could Mrs. Trelawny still enjoy herself beside the
lochs or buying Scottish plaids?

The experience had been bitter. She took it tragically. She
saw in Trelawny the responsible author of her social setback.
Why had Clarence failed to sound his parents *before* their marriage, rather than face them with a *fait accompli*? Why did he
not now insist that his legitimate wife be received by the
haughty wives of his friends? A man of good feeling can always
introduce his wife into the circle to which he belongs, and
should know how to make her acceptable to his own family!
Elizabeth Ann considered herself scorned. Trelawny had
deceived her.

Disowned in her own country, she decided to leave it and see
what welcome Paris might extend. Having duly submitted to
her period of purgatory, having married a man of good family,

---

[1] *op. cit.*, pp. 44-5 of the fifth edition (1910).

was she not henceforth in accord with the rules of a society more clement and less prudish than the Victorian world?

Most of the bachelors whom Miss Howard had once received at her table (civil servants of the Crown, young officers of the Guides and the Cent-Gardes) were now married men. The circumstances seemed favourable for taking a discreet sounding. Mr. and Mrs. Trelawny, British subjects, having decided to take up residence in France, it was but natural that they should leave cards upon those households in which the husband had been, for a long time past, on friendly relations with Mrs. Trelawny. This was in strict conformity with custom and no Parisian would have demurred had Mrs. Trelawny not once been Miss Howard!

The fear of displeasing the Empress by replying to these discreet advances with a simple mark of courtesy triumphed over politeness. Both courtiers and ladies who keep salons are pitiless. The cards left by Mr. and Mrs. Clarence Trelawny were never returned. First Scotland and now France treated them as pariahs. It was an intolerable affront.

From this time on Miss Howard was implacably bitter in her determination to be repaid by the Emperor. She was a woman who, having lost her soul and her money in a humiliating affair, had come out of it convinced of the folly of disinterested love. The Emperor's betrayal had left her wounded to the quick; her husband's unkindness made her hard. After so many heartaches, she now sought in wealth satisfactions that had nothing to do with love and, to drug herself, decided to satisfy her passion for collecting.

About this time, Napoleon III asked " how does the Howard business stand? " Mocquard gave him an account of the payments that had been made:

Note of the sums paid by the Emperor to Miss Howard, from the 24th March, 1853, to the 1st January, 1855:

The total amounts to 5,449,000 francs.

I had promised three millions plus the cost of restoring Beauregard which I estimated as being, at the most, 500,000 francs.

I gave her 1,000,000 on the 24th March, 1853, and hold the receipt.

1,500,000 on the 31st January, 1854.

1,414,000 in Government stock.

585,000 paid at the rate of 58,000 francs per month from the 1st January, 1855.

950,000 in payments of 50,000 francs from the 1st January, 1853, to the 1st January, 1855.

5,449,000 francs.[1]

In spite of this huge sum in gold francs, the unhappy woman complained that the promises made her had not been honoured. She wrote to Jean Mocquard about it. The letter quoted here is surprising for its confusion of thought, its asperity of tone and its serious faults of orthography. After living in Paris for seven years, Miss Howard had still not learnt French!

Château de Beauregard, 24 *juillet* 1855

Mon très cher ami,

Nous sommes aujourd'hui le 24 juillet et je vois avec peine que les engagements pris envers moi ne sont pas accomplis. Quand j'ai douté, j'ai blessé. Il ne pas plus se douter (*sic*). En fait, j'ai cru et je crois encore que c'est une erreur. Pourquoi me faire souffrir?

Si les choses doivent en être ainsi, j'aurais mieux fait de garder les 6 millions,—au lieu de 3.500.000 francs qui devaient, sur ma demande, être payés au bout de l'année 1853. Et c'était pour cela que j'ai prié l'Empereur de déchirer la première somme (2·500·000 francs).

Le cœur me saigne d'écrire ceci . . . *Si mon contrat de mariage n'était pas fait comme il est*, et *si je n'avais pas un enfant*, je ne ferais pas cette démarche, qui est devenue un devoir. Je compte sur vous pour faire fin à tant de souffrance!

Le cœur de l'Empereur est trop bon pour laisser une femme qu'il a aimé (*sic*) tendrement, dans une fausse position où il ne voudrait pas être lui-même . . .

[1] *Papiers et Correspondance de la famille impériale*, Vol. I, p. 172.

Vous savez ma position; vous êtes mon tuteur; et c'est à double titre que je m'adresse à vous. Je me suis trompé (*sic*) l'autre jour, en écrivant à Sa Majesté. Par une de ses lettres, date mai, il dit: " Je donnerai à Giles (*sic*) demain, papier pour les 3.500.000 francs."

Alors il né (*sic*) rien à faire que de calculer ... 50.000 depuis le 1 er juin 1853 (la rente) et 50.000 depuis janvier jusqu'à octobre.

Je prie Dieu qu'il n'en soit pas plus question d'argent entre moi et lui, qui a un tout autre sentiment dans mon cœur!

Je vous embrasse tendrement et vous aime de même.

Votre affectionnée

E. H. De Beauregard

Je vous conjure, ne laissez pas (traîner) cette lettre! Vous pouvez en faire lecture à Sa Majesté, si vous jugez convenable ... Brûlez-la aussitôt après.

J'ai vu Mme Mocquard lundi, à quatre heures ... Elle était très souffrante l'autre jour ...

Château de Beauregard, 24th July, 1855

My very dear friend,

We are to-day the 24th July and I am distressed to find that the promises made me have not been carried out. When I doubted, I wounded him. He cannot have doubted. In fact, I thought and still think that it was a mistake. Why should I be made to suffer?

If things were to turn out like this, I should have done better to keep the 6 million,—instead of the 3,500,000 francs which were to be paid me on demand at the end of the year 1853. And it was because of that that I asked the Emperor to tear up the receipt for the first sum (2,500,000 francs).

My heart bleeds to write this ... *if my marriage contract were not drawn up as it is, and if I had no child*, I would not be making this demand, which has become a duty. I count on you to put a term to my suffering!

The Emperor's heart is too kind to leave a woman whom he has tenderly loved in a false position in which he would not like to be himself ...

You know what my position is; you are my mentor; and I have a double right to address you. I made a mistake the other day when I wrote to His Majesty. In one of his letters, dated May, he says: "I will give to Giles (*sic*) to-morrow, the script for the 3,500,000 francs."

So there is nothing left for me to do but make calculations ... 50,000 since the 1st June, 1853, (interest) and 50,000 from January to October.

I pray God that there will be no further question of money between him and myself, who has quite other feelings at heart!

I embrace you tenderly and love you as always.

Your affectionate

E. H. DE BEAUREGARD

Please do not leave this letter lying about! You can read it to His Majesty, if you think proper ... Burn it immediately afterwards.

I saw Mme Mocquard on Monday at four o'clock[1] ... She was not at all well the other day ...[2]

If Miss Howard had had a librarian's experience concerning correspondence, she would have known that it suffices to write " burn this letter " in order to assure the letter's survival for ever. This is an absolute rule and the demand for money, dated 24th July, 1855, was no exception to it.

Reading this incoherent letter, at once pompous and sordid, it is difficult to believe that it came from the pen which, at the same period, was writing such gracious letters in English. Imperfection in a language sets traps for the unwary and may create insurmountable breaches between strangers.

Miss Howard's love letters have never seen the light of day. Were they destroyed? ... In this letter about money to Mocquard there is nothing but complaint and recrimination. But the friendly letters that the beautiful Englishwoman wrote to her fellow countrymen are charming and ironic in temper. Miss Ellen Stevens (a clergyman's daughter whom *Milord L'Arsouille* had taken from the family parsonage to make his

---

[1] Mme Jean Mocquard, seriously ill, was spending the summer in the country not far from Beauregard. She was to die before the end of the year, on the 18th December, 1855.

[2] *Papiers et Correspondance de la famille impériale*, Vol. I, p. 173.

mistress), Arthur Savile Grant (the inventor of newspaper kiosks), and Alfred Alderton (a first cousin with whom Mrs. Trelawny had renewed a correspondence) found in their postbox, in moments of crisis, the " Harrieteries " of which some survive. It is here that the rare and fugitive indications of an elusive character must be sought. When Mrs. Trelawny expressed herself spontaneously in her own language, she had a sense of humour, a fantastic imagination, and sometimes a sad and bitter lucidity. Hers was a fine nature, mishandled from youth and twisted by failure.

Living in France as she did, why did she never make the effort to learn French? Why did she maintain this obstinate isolationism when she was a voluntary exile? By refusing to communicate with the inhabitants of a country in which, moreover, she lived till the day of her death, Mrs. Trelawny condemned herself to relative loneliness. She made of Beauregard (Seine-et-Oise) a British enclave, open to the subjects of Queen Victoria, but without contacts with Imperial Paris. Within a completely English park, she had her rock-garden and her herbaceous borders. When Trelawny, an indefatigable traveller, was away " because he was bored," she dined alone in full evening dress, waited on by a butler and three footmen. Perhaps this rootless exile, discontented with herself and everyone else, became, in the sense in which Marcel Proust understands it, an escapist.

CHAPTER TEN

COURT INTRIGUES

EUGENIE, now married for more than three years, had not given the throne an heir. Not without a certain secret satisfaction, Mrs. Trelawny noted: " Her Majesty is beautiful, boring and barren . . ." But in this she was mistaken, for exactly at this time, Pepa Narro,[1] confidential maid, was writing in Spanish: " May God Almighty answer our prayers! Our august mistress is now in an interesting condition . . ."

The Prince Imperial, the only child of the French Sovereigns, was born on the 16th March, 1856, and his birth very nearly cost the Empress her life. Pessimistic doctors told her brutally, when she was still ill from loss of blood, that a second pregnancy would be fatal. When she had left her bed, she complained of certain physiological ills, and she underwent twice weekly a form of cauterisation. The treatment was to continue for a year. The prognostications of the doctors and her own fear of a fatal pregnancy caused her to deny the Emperor access to her bed. Their married love became platonic to which Eugénie, who had a lust for power, soon added a political twist. She often thought of becoming Regent and she was, in fact, to be appointed as such during the war of Italian independence. To her old friend Mérimée, she one day made the melancholy confidence,

---

[1] Josefa Narro, called Pepa, at one time maid to the Comtesse de Montijo, was in charge of the Empress's wardrobe at the Tuileries and became her confidante. " She prospered by taking exorbitant commissions and from various other illicit sources." She married a French officer called Pollet, whom the Empress had made a Colonel in the Voltigeurs of the Guard, and who was killed in 1870.

"There is now no longer any *Ugénie*. There is only the Empress."

"Glory is a transcendant mourning for happiness," said Mme de Staël. Had Eugénie been happy and in love, would she have wished to reign? . . . Napoleon III openly deceived her. After the "English chain" and the Spanish marriage, this xenophile Don Juan had two Italian liaisons, one with Virginia Oldolni, "the divine Comtesse" de Castiglione, and the other with Marie-Anne de Ricci, whom Walewski had just married as his second wife.

In the name of the unity of the peninsula, Cavour had given Virginia, his near relation, orders to please the Emperor of the French, who was an indispensable ally. Her mission having been fulfilled, the Empress took umbrage. At the fancy-dress ball given by the Minister for Foreign Affairs (17th February, 1856), the triumphant woman had dared appear dressed as the Queen of Hearts before the Empress who was then "quite round" since she was eight months gone in her pregnancy. The Queen of Hearts wears a gown of the utmost decency, but Virginia had conceived something more provocatively décolleté. A girdle accented the extreme slimness of her waist; attached to it was a purse in the form of a heart which hung below her belt. Having examined her rival's appearance, the Empress said coldly in the hearing of the whole Court: "Her heart is rather low."

Lord Cowley complained that the Emperor, "so much engrossed and occupied with the beauteous Castiglione," was difficult of access, having postponed an audience with the impatient diplomat. "The latter is a decided liaison and carried on at the Élysée. It will do his nerves no good."

Dr. Ferguson, called in consultation, had indeed informed the British Ambassador that the Emperor, old before his time, suffered from debility due to his daily excesses of work and sensuality.

Lord Cowley to Lord Clarendon: "Great alterations of character may take place—apathy, irritation, caprice, infirmity of purpose are upon the cards, as the result of an exhausted nervous system and diseased organs. The political results of this may be fearful and we may soon have to make great allowances for physical infirmity. Ferguson, very properly, keeps the matter a profound secret, and I believe has not told Persigny more than half the truth.

Lord Clarendon replied: " I am very sorry for the Castiglione affair because it will damage the Emperor, and still more because it must annoy the Empress. I have no doubt the lady fulfils all the conditions of *coquine*. Do keep me *au courant* of the affair." [1]

After the baptism of the Prince Imperial, the Empress left for Biarritz and the Emperor went to take the waters in the Vosges.

Lord Cowley to Lord Clarendon, 1st July, 1856: " The Emperor is off to Plombières . . . Care has been taken for His Majesty's *menus plaisirs* and a *lady* is already installed there. In the meantime, all Paris is scandalised by His Majesty's late proceedings with the Castiglione. Even the Court entourage talk of a *fête champêtre* the other night at Villeneuve-l'Étang, where a few select were alone invited and where His Majesty rowed the said lady in a small boat alone and then disappeared with her in certain dark walks during the whole of the evening. The poor Empress was in a sad state —got excited and began to dance, when not being sufficiently strong she fell very heavily. It was a regular orgy, the men dancing with their hats on. All this is very sad. It does the Emperor an infinity of harm politically speaking . . ." [2]

Without ever having seen " the beauteous Castiglione," Mrs. Trelawny shared the Empress's concern. Pretending not to know what the new favourite was called, she asked Lord Hertford, " Do you know the woman? . . . You know the one I mean, the woman whose name is like a street?"

Upon which Lord Henry Seymour, quicker than his brother with a witty reply, cried, " What do you mean by that, my dear? Is it *Vide-Gousset* or *Git-le Cœur*?"

[1] *The Paris Embassy during the Second Empire*, Lord Cowley's papers, pp. 95–6.
[2] *The Paris Embassy during the Second Empire*, Lord Cowley's papers, p. 102.

Intriguing, grasping and not very clever, the divine Comtesse quickly fell from grace. " I have hardly begun to live and yet my part is already played! " she wrote at the age of twenty-three. Avid for jewels, she had made the Emperor give her " an emerald worth a hundred thousand francs, the most beautiful in the world," if one is to believe the Duchesse de Dino, who moreover adds: " Mme de Castiglione, whose reign is over, is returning to Piedmont, bearing with her the colossal emerald." [1]

Marie-Anne Walewska, " a tiny beauty, blonde as March corn," loved her husband so much that, in order to assure him a dazzling career and a huge fortune, she took the Emperor as her lover. She came from the Florentine nobility and was as cunning as she was beautiful.

" I do not know," said Mérimée, " if it is true, as she claims, that her family originates with Machiavelli; what is certain is that *she* is descended from him."

Mistress of Napoleon III and wife of the Minister for Foreign Affairs, she had the remarkable tact to ingratiate herself with the Empress. " Mme Walewska is her greatest friend," wrote Guizot to Laure de Gasparin, " which does not prevent what you have been told from being true, and much else besides! " Eugénie always pretended to believe that there could be nothing more in the relationship between her august husband and her " very dear little Marie " than innocent and brotherly comradeship. Perhaps she felt that a rapid succession of passing fancies would be less dangerous to the equilibrium of her own marriage than an enduring affection such as Miss Howard had once inspired? " It is said," Guizot wrote again, " that the Empress, concerned about Mme de Castiglione, has used Mme Walewska to set her aside, and is now seeking someone with whom to set aside Mme Walewska . . ." [2]

The conservative attitude of the husband, Walewski, was

---

[1] Duchesse de Dino, *Chronique*, Vol. IV, pp. 250–3.
[2] Letters quoted by André Gayot in *François Guizot et Madame Laure de Gasparin*, pp. 467–8 and 542.

precisely calculated to appeal to a Catholic sovereign. We have already seen that Eugénie delighted in politics. She supported the idea that the maintenance of temporal power was necessary to the prestige and independence of the Holy See. When Napoleon III wished to liberate Italy from the Austrian yoke, Eugénie realised that the papal states were threatened; she prayed the Walewskis to join her in opposing so sacrilegious a war. Thus the Emperor was opposed by a party whose leaders were his wife, his mistress and his Minister for Foreign Affairs.

If the Empress had adopted " the little Walewska " to the extent of making her an intimate friend, Mme de Beauregard was, on the contrary, furiously hostile to her. Far removed from these conspiracies, she nevertheless remained curious and concerned about them.

By his liaison with Marie Walewska, Napoleon I had had a son, Comte Alexandre, the husband of a second Marie Walewska. Were all the women of this name inevitably destined for the Imperial bed? " It's a family tradition," noted Mrs. Trelawny. " The Foreign Secretary urged his wife to follow in his own mother's footsteps. No wonder if she practises what her lord and master preaches. Each reigning Bonaparte must sleep with a Walewska . . ." [1]

The bitter letter-writer's marriage with Trelawny was not going well; she accused him of exploiting her. " He costs too much," she wrote to Strode, " I don't want to be to him the hen that lays the golden eggs." Perhaps Elizabeth Ann would have done better to have attached this fickle husband to herself even at the cost of a few feathers? In these early quarrels of their marriage, the fault was not all on Clarence's side.

Though she had a perfect steward at Beauregard, named Jean Duboz, Mrs. Trelawny had brought her cousin Alfred Alderton from England who, she said, would perform the functions of an accountant. To complete her estate, she desired to acquire certain lands on its boundaries and wished that her transactions

[1] Unpublished letter. Private collection.

131

in real estate should be negotiated by an agent who would look competently after her interests. When Alderton became her accountant he had, in fact, the right of supervising all Trelawny's expenditure. The latter, fearing that the cousin had been brought over merely in order to keep watch upon him, paid him every possible mark of disrespect.

He also found Mrs. Trelawny's snobbery extremely irritating. When he had asked for Miss Howard's hand in Florence, the latter had thought that their marriage would make her *Lady* Trelawny. The younger son of a cadet branch, Clarence could not give her a title which belonged by right only to his aunt, and he had frankly explained the genealogical situation. When, later, the châtelaine of Beauregard ordered her servants to call her *My lady*, Trelawny had no wish to contradict her in the presence of her household but whenever, in an hotel or a shop, she usurped the title, he showed his displeasure.

Then, out of vanity, she committed the worst possible blunder: since she could not be Lady Trelawny, she became, more than ever, Comtesse de Beauregard and had the coat of arms the Emperor had given her put up everywhere: Azur, a dove argent, bearing in its beak an olive branch verte; in chief or three ivy leaves verte.[1]

When this became known in Paris, Mérimée said, " Here's the eagle distributing doves ! "

Elizabeth Ann had need of the social support that the " gentleman from Cornwall " could alone assure her. In disdaining the condition of wife to the younger son of a good family, Clarence Trelawny, Esq., merely, though an authentic member of the landed gentry, she succeeded in making her humiliated husband into an enemy prepared to do her a bad turn, into an adversary

---

[1] See *Titres et Confirmations de Titres* by the Vicomte Révérend, Vol. XI of his *Armorial*, p. 351. Not knowing of the existence of the letter of the 24th January, 1853, which was in England, Révérend denies Miss Howard's ennoblement. " If the fact were true," he writes, " there would be traces of it to be found in the Archives of the Sceau de France, and the decree in favour of the son indicates the surname of *Beauregard* rather than that of *Béchevêt*." The question was in reality more complex.

who was inclined to speak ill of her. Why did she consider it a point of honour to reject an honourable name which, once given, could not be taken from her? Why did she wish to call herself Comtesse de Beauregard, when she was only half a Comtesse and no relation whatever to the authentic houses of Beauregard? Solidly based in marriage and leading—as indeed she did from the date the unfaithful Emperor left her—an impeccable life, she would have ended, as time went on, in forcing an entry into that society which was now closed to her. The attractive and fantastic woman's actions are always unexpected and frequently unintelligible. Her obstinacy in living, and dying, under a false name increased the ambiguity of her position, lent it a character proper only to an adventuress.

Her life, full of aberrations and errors, was to be overshadowed by profound sorrow. The Treasurer-General to the Crown married the woman he loved and by whom he had a child on the 3rd August, 1858. On that day, Pierre Bure and Alexandrine Vergeot recognised and legitimised not only their son Pierre Alexandre, but, in addition, Louis and Eugène. The same civil document regularised the position of " the beautiful clog dancer " and transformed her three bastards into the legitimate sons of a high functionary.

The family, united from now on, had their particular rank to maintain in Second Empire Society. Mme Bure, now promoted to the French upper middle class, demanded, as might be expected, that Louis and Eugène should be returned to her. In vain did their guardian object that the children had been confided to her by the Emperor and that, for ten long years, she had cherished them. Alas, a sentimental argument has no value in the eyes of the law. The minors in the case were not consulted. Mrs. Trelawny might call herself " their adopted mother," but M. Bure was incontestably their father according to law. In measured terms, though they give an authentic impression of despair, Elizabeth Ann addressed her complaints to an English counsellor:

I am in sorrow. The terrible ordeal of parting from my beloved boys shall be my undoing. I cannot help thinking this might have been prevented, for pity's sake, had Someone wanted to spare me. I remember so well the day when the Prince entrusted his children to my care. I was so glad that I shouted: " Louis, I have three sons now! " He looked happy and said, with a kind smile: " Thank you, dear. In other words say *we* have three sons," and I am sure he meant it. Unfortunately, I have not met His Majesty for years, and now Mme Bure wants her whole family to look respectable. Honestly, am I not worth Mme Bure? When we were both unmarried, she was glad to get rid of her first-born children. I reared them; I mothered them; I never charged a farthing for their upkeep as long as the Prince was hard-up (that is in his Presidency days) . . .

Anyhow, let us all do as he pleases. His will be done in Beauregard as it is in Paris. God bless the Emperor! He that can do no wrong probably knows best. Whatever he enforces, I shall love him till I die.

To lessen the shock, Mrs. Trelawny was promised that she should frequently see her " beloved boys." In fact, they very soon ceased visiting her. Alexandrine, jealous of the foreigner, denigrated her with hypocritical refinements. Eugène was fifteen; Louis, thirteen; they were at an age which lacks perception. The two boys were perhaps really attached to their foster-mother but they were easily influenced; they got tired of hearing her called a hussy and gave up defending her in order not to hear her spoken of. Elizabeth Ann, shut up in Beauregard, lost sight of them completely.

CHAPTER ELEVEN

THE LONELY CHÂTEAU

THE DESIRE to live a retired, dignified and decent life became an obsession with Mrs. Trelawny. In order to defend herself against undesirable curiosity, she wished to enclose within high walls the block consisting of Beauregard, Béchevêt, Bel-Ébat, and the meadows of Orient, Gresset and some others. She did not like strangers having the right to walk upon her land, by roads that were rights-of-way, but how could she stop people using the public highway?

The Commune of La Celle-Saint-Cloud was, as was only to be expected, hostile to her plan. The Comtesse de Beauregard brought into play the high authorities of the Civil List. She was the owner of the woods which separated the forest of Marly-le-Roi from the park of Saint-Cloud and offered them to the Crown in exchange for permission to build at her own expense two carriage roads which were to pass round the outside of her estate instead of through it. This done, she could build the wall which was to ensure her privacy. It was to have five monumental gates flanked by lodges. The construction of this wall alone cost eight hundred thousand gold francs (£160,000 of modern money). To satisfy her taste for mystery and in order to enclose herself within a fortified camp, Elizabeth Ann was prepared to spend money with incredible prodigality.

She was hardly more than thirty when she made the decision to spend the rest of her life behind walls which made of her estate an invisible domain. In choosing solitude, she was abandoning herself to a strange malady of mind and body. This would not have been perceptible to a casual observer, since her beauty remained intact and her reserve stoically English. But her poetic reverie was shot with an appalling bitterness. From an obscure childhood she had hoisted herself on to the boards of the theatre and, from there, an irresistible force had projected her on to the steps of a throne. But the steps only . . .

The impetus once lost, the climber was to climb no higher. Alone in a world that was a prey to political upheaval, she learned to know hardness of heart, imposture and betrayal. From her battle with mankind, she retained a despairing scepticism, a cynicism veiled with irony and an unrelieved discouragement.

Once delighting in theatres, balls and horse-racing, the beauty in the sleeping park went to the other extreme and determined never to show herself in Paris again. All was vanity! . . . She mourned her great love and renounced all vain pretension. The Emperor had completely forgotten her. Good people withheld from her their esteem. The paradise reserved for great men, pure women, legitimate children, and girls with handsome dowries, the world peopled with upright bourgeoisie, happy marriages and matrons of unimpeachable propriety was a universe fortified, defended at all points, against the invasion of beautiful penitents. Miss Howard, realising that she would never be admitted into it, chose flight from her century.

What is admirable is that, having decided to live hidden at Beauregard, she persevered in her sombre intention. She still had ten years to live. She spent them in complete retirement. Some people found it extraordinary that no one ever heard speak of Harriet Howard any more. But even the usual Parisian malice never attributed to her a single liaison after her marriage. Her memory soon faded even from the recollections of the chroniclers of the time. In the memoirs of the period, in private journals, her name disappears, all track of her is lost . . . Some of her old friends said that she had returned to England, or gone to America.

Others thought she was already dead and others again said that she had gone mad and had been shut up.

Certain English residents in Paris, few but faithful, still went to visit the recluse. Lord Hertford, whom she called " the Dean of my friends," was assiduous. Lord Henry Seymour, his brother, and Richard Wallace, the Marquess's only and illegitimate son, were no less so. When they went to Beauregard, they took their mistresses with them.

Lord Hertford had had as mistress for the last twenty years, a woman of great culture and distinction: Louise-Suzanne Bréart. The daughter of a French professor and sister of an inspector of schools, Mlle Bréart called herself " Mme Oger " from respect for a university family to whom her irregular liaison caused shame and despair. " In a more righteous world," wrote Bernard Falk, the historian of the Seymour family, " this highly accomplished and victimised lady would have been the legal Marchioness of Hertford . . . She would have proved an admirable wife and was, in every respect, a worthy consort for a gentleman of culture . . ." [1] Unfortunately for Mlle Bréart, the gentleman was a Seymour and therefore a libertine.

He had met her in Paris in 1834. Louise Bréart was, at that time, a ravishing, ingenuous and fanciful girl. The idea of a romantic elopement, followed by a secret marriage, must have tempted the credulous child. It was a question, said her seducer, of evading the watchfulness of a family that was too middle-class not to be suspicious. They must leave for England, where a clergyman was already waiting to bless the fugitives' union.

The imprudent Louise had taken the risk and made the journey. " The evening they arrived in London she was taken to a house where a marriage ceremony was duly gone through and what appeared to be a register signed . . ." [2] Alas, two months later, Lord Hertford, whose valet, disguised as a clergyman, had played

[1] Bernard Falk, *Old Q's Daughter*, pp. 209 and 294.
[2] Bernard Falk, op cit., p. 301.

the part of officiating priest, admitted to the horrified Louise that it had been " a mock marriage."

As victim of a sacrilegious parody, she could have brought and won a case of breach of promise. But, madly in love with the impostor, she resigned herself, in order not to have to leave him, to the humiliations of concubinage. Always dressed from head to foot in white (which she continued to do to the age of eighty), active, intelligent and kind, she played the part of hostess at Sudbourn Hall in Suffolk, Bagatelle in the Seine and other enchanting places. Old Lady Hertford treated her as *de facto*, if not *de jure*, daughter-in-law and always showed her esteem and affection. Mlle Bréart's noble qualities, her irreproachable fidelity to the man who, having once betrayed her confidence, frequently took pleasure in deceiving her, were certainly moving titles to the dignity of peeress which was constantly denied her. The noble lord must have loved her in his haughty and egoistical way, since their relationship lasted until his death thirty-six years later; but he never legally married her.

When she besought him to legalise her position, he replied that there was another very old friend who had, like her and for a longer period, the right to a regular position. It was true. Until his death, the fourth Lord Hertford kept, as he said, " two official mistresses without counting casual ones."

At Oxford, George Idle, the son of the Member of Parliament for Weymouth, had been his friend. George Idle had died young, leaving a pretty widow to be consoled. The mistress with a prior claim over Mlle Bréart was this Mrs. George Idle, née Amelia Collins. She was maintained all her life by the cynical Hertford, though the latter rarely saw her and it was " Mme Oger " who accompanied him upon all his travels.

An Englishwoman, much younger than Louise Bréart, accompanied Lord Henry to Beauregard. It was that clergyman's daughter of whom he had made a lost sheep. In 1852, Ellen Stevens had presented him with a daughter who, for lack of her father's name, bore the two Christian names of her grandmother, Lady Hertford: Maria Emily. "Out of respect for the decencies" and following the example of Mlle Bréart, Miss Stevens had also given herself a married name under the pseudonym of Mrs. Minchin.

It will not have been forgotten that, since 1839, Richard Wallace had been having an affair with Julie Castelnau. It is nevertheless impossible to imagine two people less suited to each other. Wallace had the culture and distinction of a great lord; Julie, the natural impetuosity of a brazen ignoramus. He delighted in the beautiful and the antique; she was passionately fond of the modern style and was only interested in objects of practical utility. The delicacy of a man full of heart was in contrast to the bluntness of a silly egoist. This ill-assorted couple was nevertheless to prove itself indissoluble over more than half a century. Richard Wallace had ideas upon the duty of a decent man that were utterly different to those his father and his Uncle Henry held. He would have liked to increase the happiness of the human race. The feeling of responsibility he had towards the woman who had made him a father, prevented his ever leaving her, shrewish, ignorant and narrow as she was; her one quality seems to have been a rather mean economy.

The Marchioness of Hertford, a kindly dowager, who had taken a liking to Louise Bréart, her son's mistress, could never put up with the vulgarity of Julie Castelnau, the mistress of her grandson. At Beauregard, Elizabeth Ann, observing the three women, concluded that the least amiable was the most loved. She herself thought sadly of the past: the man who owed her a throne had abandoned her, the most beautiful of women who was passionately devoted to him.

What ought she to have done to retain and hold his constancy? How was Julie better qualified to inspire a lasting affection? Mrs. Trelawny asked herself these questions in vain. What would she have said if she could have imagined the then unfore-

[1] Jean Stern, *Lord Seymour, dit Milord l'Arsouille*, pp. 215-20.

seeable future, in which Lady Wallace, née Castelnau, was to enter the English aristocracy and there be treated with the respect due to her husband's rank?

It was under the influence of Lord Hertford, a passionate lover of art, that Miss Howard had early acquired a taste for pictures and porcelain. When she bought tapestries and period furniture for Beauregard, Richard Wallace gave her intelligent advice. A philanthropist, he was, as the whole world knows to-day, a born collector. Much occupied with social work, he incited Mrs. Trelawny to turn from politics to charity. In particular, he persuaded her to rescue and bring up at Beauregard a little French orphan girl, Octavie d'Espinassy. Elizabeth Ann became attached to the girl and, a few years later, gave a party to celebrate her engagement to Alfred Alderton. In spite of her own personal setbacks, Mrs. Trelawny believed in marriage.

Louise Bréart, Ellen Stevens and Julie Castelnau enjoyed visiting the hot-houses at Beauregard and walking with their hostess in the peaceful gardens invisible to the common herd. Of these four women encased in crinolines, huge beribboned hats upon their heads, Mlle Bréart was the only one not to have had a natural child; Mrs. Trelawny alone had been married. Elizabeth Ann's past, her ineffaceable past, condemned her to friendships only with women outside society. She herself said, with a bitter wryness: "I am not received by honest women and their unblemished daughters see in me the last of the prostitutes! . . ." It was, unfortunately, only too true.

Martin was painfully aware of the situation. As soon as he was old enough to understand it, he became ashamed of his mother and showed it. Because she had a great deal to be forgiven, Elizabeth Ann overwhelmed the spoiled disdainful child with presents and treats. As soon as Martin expressed a wish, it was immediately fulfilled. To see a smile of content upon that face which so much resembled her own, she was prepared to go to any lengths. Educated by a series of remarkable tutors, destined for a diplomatic career, the boy (protected by the

Emperor, who wished him well) was received by a world into which his mother had never gained admittance. That he might shine in it, she gave him the most beautiful saddle horses available, and sent him to a fashionable tailor who dressed him as a "dandy." In the space of a few years, " she had succeeded in creating a boy who was at once charming and odious." Having no qualifications to read him moral lessons, she did not dare check his laziness and prodigality. When he acquired a fatal taste for cards, she paid his gaming debts without reproach. Martin was her one pride; perhaps, too, he was her worst weakness. A more disciplined upbringing would have obtained better results.

Ever since he had been told the history of Miss Howard, young Béchevêt pursued the single objective of an important marriage, one whose brilliance would make people forget his origins. Rich and extremely good-looking, he might with the aid of providence and the Emperor of the French well aspire to it. But would the daughter of an aristocratic family accept the too-notorious Harriet Howard as mother-in-law? It was to be doubted. As Alexandre Dumas *fils* cruelly said, the reformed *demi-mondaine* " was only a comtesse to her servants and her tradesmen." Alas, the mere existence of such a mother was a handicap to the son's future.

As had the young Vergeots (become Bure), Martin left Beauregard. Elizabeth Ann, in despair, saw him but rarely. She literally played the part of a *Mère Goriot*, disavowed, held at arm's length, but prepared for any heroic sacrifice that might be needed to assure her son a happy life.

One of her English friends, Arthur Savile Grant, was witness to her struggles. During her ten expiatory years, he stayed frequently with the repentant sinner. Beauregard in those days had fewer visitors than it had butlers, cooks, housemaids, laundry-maids, gardeners, postillions and grooms. Sometimes the hostess hired a chamber orchestra from Paris so that her reader and her single guest might be regaled with music. She managed the Bel-Ébat stud competently, but no longer went to the races. Trelawny, on the other hand, took his stepson to Newmarket, Goodwood and Chantilly.

In these years 1855–65, Beauregard was almost a forerunner of the Bavarian castles that Ludwig II, the mad king, was to build in order to live in solitude with his ghosts. Though on a smaller scale, the orchestras hired to give a musical evening to three people sitting in a huge empty room make one think of the Wagnerian performances which the narcissitic Hamlet II had performed in an empty theatre long before he became the victim of hallucination, madness and suicide ... In the case of the young Harriet Howard, who invented poetic myths about a wholly imaginary past to " recompense herself for the injustices of fate," was there not a mild form of dementia præcox? Fairy tales do not necessarily dissolve at the hour of awakening. With some people dreams can last all day, even all their lives.

Death was to deprive Elizabeth Ann of her most faithful friends. Lord Henry Seymour died the first, at fifty-four years of age, on the 16th October, 1859. Founder of the *Society for Encouraging the Improvement of the Breeding of Horses in France*, he had also, he said, contributed to the improvement of the breed of the human race by selecting beautiful women with whom to make half-Seymours. The products of this breeding, whether foals or babies, were equally dear to him. " I wish," can be read in the will of *Milord L'Arsouille*, " that the horses known to my friends as being my favourites should be kept in some place where they will be exempt from all work and well-cared for ..."[1] By leaving a large sum for the maintenance of these old horses, the testator spared them the horrors of hippophagy.

This happy bachelor had had six surviving children by four different mothers. He divided his worldly goods among his bastards whose mothers, *on condition that they never married*, were to receive pensions for life. Three other mistresses, who had remained childless, nevertheless received life annuities. The

[1] cf. Jean Stern, *Lord Seymour, dit Milord L'Arsouille*, p. 260.

old stallion chose Richard Wallace as executor of his last will and testament. A considerable part of the inheritance was destined for hospitals in London and Paris; *Milord L'Arsouille*, though dissolute, was charitable.

Jean Mocquard, who had now long been a widower, had, so he said, " one foot in the grave." Mrs. Trelawny, who called him " her tutor," sent every day for news of him to the Tuileries, where the Emperor had provided his devoted servant with a grace and favour apartment. As long as Mocquard was alive, Miss Howard preserved the illusion of some invisible, hidden, but nevertheless real, link between the unforgettable past and the overcast present. Once Mocquard died, all hope would be gone.

Elizabeth Ann clung to the ruins of past happiness, but such vestiges of walls that still remained standing after the earthquake were, one by one, to founder. She herself was ill of a cancer. The mere thought of a surgical operation horrified her. To persuade her, the doctors insisted without concealment upon the extreme gravity of her case.

The Empress also had her sorrows. Her much beloved sister was suffering from an incurable disease of the spinal marrow. On the 16th September, 1860, Paca, having come to France for treatment, died there in a hotel, during an official journey of the Sovereigns in Algeria. By order of Napoleon III, the fatal news was kept secret from the Empress in order that, unaware of her mourning, she should take part in all the African functions with a smiling face.

The august couple were quarrelling more than ever. Two months after the death of the Duchess of Alba, the Foreign Secretary was informed by Lord Cowley that the Empress of the French would leave on the following morning for Scotland. An inexplicable decision. Why should this chilly Spaniard suddenly wish to visit Edinburgh at the worst time of the year?

Lord Cowley to Lord Clarendon, 13th November, 1860: " Various motives are attributed to this somewhat extraordinary proceeding

—grief—ill health—jealousy. The Emperor says that the Empress's nerves are in such a state that she will not recover nor resume her usual avocations until after an absence. Some people say that she is suffering from the same disease that killed her sister, and that she wants to consult *privately* Dr. Simpson of Edinburgh. Lastly it is whispered that the presence of the beautiful Madame de Castiglione at Paris has something to do with Her Majesty's absence . . ." [1]

Arrived in London, the improvident Empress, who had forgotten to reserve rooms, had to go from hotel to hotel. It was only at the fifth attempt that she succeeded in finding suitable accommodation. " The Emperor was delighted when he heard this and laughed heartily," wrote Lord Cowley. The Ambassador reported that he had it from unimpeachable sources that the flight to Scotland had followed " terrible scenes, made by the Empress, on the subject of the papacy." Eugénie had, so he said, threatened her husband, whom she called a *heretic*, with the divine wrath and the most appalling torments in this world and the next.

Lord Clarendon, after an audience with Queen Victoria, replied to Lord Cowley:

" Her Majesty was much occupied about the Empress's journey and was as little able as any of her subjects to understand it. It was generally thought to have been arranged with the Duchess of Hamilton, who, however, knew so little about it that when she heard of the intention to come to Scotland, she telegraphed to the Emperor to know if it was true, and to hope the Empress would come to Hamilton. The answer was rather an odd one to send openly: ' *L'Impératrice est fort souffrante, surtout moralement. Elle est en Écosse. Je doute fort qu'elle puisse aller à Hamilton.*'

" She wrote a most proper letter to the Queen which I saw, expressing a hope that she might be allowed to see her, when she returned from Scotland. The Queen is most kindly disposed and means to do whatever the Empress likes. They have heard through Persigny that she wishes to go to Windsor."

[1] *The Paris Embassy during the Second Empire*, Lord Cowley's papers, p. 211.

The interview between the Sovereigns took place a month later. Lord Clarendon wrote of it to Lord Cowley: " The Queen remarked that the Empress's manner was the same as usual, though it was rather shy, adding that she had not even indirectly alluded to the Emperor . . ." [1] Every court in Europe was wondering what could have caused so unprecedented a journey. From the castle of Laeken, the King of the Belgians wrote his thoughts upon it to his niece:

The King of the Belgians to Queen Victoria, 22nd November, 1860: " Eugénie's expedition is most astonishing. She coughs much, and I never heard Scotland recommended for Winter excursions. I believe that the death of her sister affected her a good deal. She seems to have been a good deal *choquée* that she had been dancing in Africa when that poor sister was dying. Next to this, there seems a difference of opinion with her master on the subject of the Pope . . ." [2]

Queen Victoria to the King of the Belgians, 4th December, 1860: " The Empress came at half-past one, and stayed till a little after three. She looked very pretty, but very sad—and in speaking of her health and of her return from Algiers began to cry. She seems to be much better, however, for her journey; before she could neither eat nor sleep, nor would she take notice of anything. She never mentioned the Emperor . . . It is altogether very strange . . ."

11th December, 1860: " The Empress is still here, and enjoys her liberty of *all* things. We went to town for the Smithfield Cattle Show yesterday, and visited her at Claridge's Hotel. She very civilly wanted us to avoid the trouble, but we felt that it would not be civil if we did not, and that hereafter even the French might say that she had not been treated with due respect. She looked very pretty, and was in very good spirits, but again carefully avoided any allusion to her husband . . ." [3]

[1] Op cit., pp. 213–14.
[2] *The letters of Queen Victoria,* Vol. III, p. 415.
[3] *The letters of Queen Victoria,* Vol. III, pp. 418–19.

CHAPTER TWELVE

ELIZABETH ANN TRELAWNY, COMTESSE DE BEAUREGARD

ON THE 16th November, 1861, a sick woman made her will:

" This is the last Will of me, Elizabeth Ann Trelawny, now the wife of Clarence Trelawny, Esquire, formerly Elizabeth Ann Haryett, Comtesse de Beauregard in France: which Will I make in pursuance of the several powers and authorities to me given or reserved, by virtue of a settlement made previously to my marriage with the said Clarence Trelawny Esquire, and dated the 15th day of May, 1854 . . .

" First I appoint Nathaniel William John Strode (who is one of the trustees of such settlement), and Captain Charles Simon Lousada, a former officer in the British Army . . .

" I hereby give and bequeath, so far as the law of France will allow this, my Will, to operate thereon, all my estate of Beauregard, in France; and all my estate in the Champs-Élysées, near Paris; and all my other real, and all my personal estate and effects of every nature and kind, in the Empire of France, unto Martin Constantine Haryett de Beauregard, in my said settlement mentioned and described absolutely."

Here Elizabeth Ann, writing at interminable length in her maternal tongue, had prudently added: " It is my intention to confirm this bequest by a will executed according to the French law," but either through negligence or exhaustion she made no further effort to study the differences in the law of succession in the two neighbouring countries, and the second will, which was to conform to the Code Napoléon, was never made.

What was surprising was that the " Countess de Beauregard in France," born in Sussex, expressed the formal wish to be buried outside of either France or England: " I direct that my funeral shall take place in Scotland, in the simplest possible manner, at the Grey Friars Church, Edinburgh . . ." There are no posthumous explanations of this curious choice; it is one mystery the more.

After eleven pages of legacies there follows:

" I give to Melliora Findon, of the Château de Beauregard, spinster, an annuity of one hundred pounds during her life.—And I give to my friend, Mademoiselle Octavie d'Espinassy of Château de Beauregard, an annuity of fifty pounds during her life—And I also give to each of them, the said Melliora Findon and Octavie d'Espinassy, the sum of fifty pounds for mourning . . ."

Special dispositions were made in view of the recent engagement celebrated at Beauregard,

" as to the sum of twenty thousand pounds, directed to be appropriated for the benefit of my cousin Alfred Alderton, I direct that my trustees shall cause a settlement to be made . . . and shall thereby secure the income of the said fund, for the benefit of Alfred Alderton (and his wife), for his life and after his death, in case an intended marriage between Alfred Alderton and Mademoiselle Octavie d'Espinassy shall take effect . . ."

The Executors of the will were not forgotten:

" I give to Nathaniel William John Strode, one of the trustees of my marriage settlement, the sum of one thousand pounds; and the gold repeater watch with my Arms engraved; and the gold chain which I always wear, as a remembrance of his kind services to me.—And to Captain Charles Simon Lousada, an annuity of two thousand pounds, payable to him during his life, and my portrait by Edward Moira."

The kindness once shown to "little Bess" by an understanding relation now bore fruit:

"I give to my aunt Frances Alderton an annuity of one hundred pounds *per annum*, payable to her during her life and, in case she shall die leaving her husband, Charles Alderton, surviving her, then after her decease I give to the said Charles Alderton an annuity of sixty pounds during the residue of his life ... I give to my old housekeeper, Sarah Spriggs, an annuity of forty pounds during her life ... And I give an annuity of forty pounds to Guillaume Fodor, an artist of 1, Albany Chambers, London, during his life ... And I give to Colonel William Ridley a legacy of one hundred pounds, as a souvenir; and to Captain Howard Wyse a like sum of one hundred pounds, also as a souvenir ... I give Madame Hugon, my housekeeper, one hundred pounds to purchase her a place in *Les Petits Ménages*, Paris ... I give ... I give ... I give ..."

There are certain passages in the long will which assist the understanding of the testator's character. Other paragraphs cast light on sombre corners of her past. For instance, it is to be remembered that Miss Howard's love life began with a romantic elopement followed by an appalling disillusionment. And here is her expressed intention that the rest of her fortune, after the various legacies had been paid and the annuities had terminated, should go to the founding of a refuge for unfortunate females:

"There shall be founded and established (by and out of such funds) a Charity, or charitable Institution which shall bear my name, the object and purport of such charity being for the purpose of reclaiming, and affording a home for, and teaching a trade to unfortunate females who may have been seduced from their family homes and be repentant. I wish and desire that a good education be afforded, they being taught (if deficient) reading, writing, arithmetic, etc. .... No girl can be maintained and supported at the expense of such charity longer than two years, unless she be judged, by the Committee of Management, to be useful as an instructress ..." [1]

[1] From an unpublished will in the possession of Maître Mahot de La Quérantonnais.

The staff of the Château de Beauregard were recompensed. Every servant who had spent more than five years in her service received a small legacy. But, before unconsciousness and death overtook her, Elizabeth Ann had still to solve a question to which her son attached great importance. It much displeased the young Béchevêt (an authentic comte since the Imperial decree) that the material possessions of his mother, now known to be dying, should be indissolubly joined by marriage to those of Clarence Trelawny.

At that period, divorce existed in England, but it was not to be re-established in France till the Naquet law of twenty years later. Martin insisted that his mother should at least be legally separated and, since Mrs. Trelawny had just cause to show, the Civil Tribunal released her from marital control. Béchevêt would have liked her to obtain a complete dissolution of her unfortunate marriage in London. But there was an insurmountable difficulty. Only British subjects, domiciled in the United Kingdom, could apply for divorce in the courts. For many years Mrs. Trelawny had lived far from her own land; she no longer possessed even the shadow of a residential qualification. To take her case to law, she would have had to become resident in London and live there a certain time. She was too ill to make the idea of such an uprooting tolerable. The divorce proposal was abandoned.

Being unable to get rid of his stepfather, Martin manœuvred to obtain certain personal advantages by agreement. The proof of an agreement between the two men exists to-day in the archives of Maître Mahot de La Quérantonnais, great-grandson and direct successor of the lawyer Amédée Mocquard, with whom Mrs. Trelawny's will was lodged. The documents (which were kindly placed at my disposal) contain a deed by which Clarence Trelawny cedes to the Comte de Béchevêt his rights of co-proprietorship upon certain properties acquired, jointly with his wife, in the Avenue des Champs Élysées. A profitable cession, for it liberated a part of the real estate which the young Comte was to inherit from the Trelawny lien.

As her health grew worse, her relations with her husband deteriorated. The will of 1861 still left Trelawny certain benefits. A document, dated 29th March, 1864, disinherited him:

"This is a Codicil to the last Will and Testament of me, Elizabeth Ann Trelawny, wife of Clarence Trelawny, Esquire, formerly Elizabeth Haryett and Countess de Beauregard in France, which will bears date on (or about) the sixteenth day of November 1861, and is made in pursuance of the several powers and authorities therein referred to . . . Now I do hereby, in pursuance of every power and authority in me vested, absolutely revoke and make void every appointment and gift, by way of annuity or otherwise, by my will, made to (or in favour of) my said husband, Clarence Trelawny. And I do further appoint, and give to, and in favour of Martin Constantine Haryett de Beauregard, in my said will named,—and who is now authorized in France to bear the name and title of Count de Béchevêt, all such gifts and interests as, under my said will, my husband would (but for this codicil) have been entitled to take . . ." [1]

Mrs. Trelawny not only wished to assure her son's future, she also wished to make sure that he would not be accused of ingratitude. In her correspondence of the years 1864–65, she hardly refers to any other topic but the young diplomatic attaché:

The Countess of Beauregard to Captain Lousada: "Martin visits me, not frequently, but occasionally. I cannot blame him for it. All his smart friends speak ill of me and call me names. How could he bring them here, on Sundays? . . . Flowers from my conservatories are sent, with his card, to ladies who would rather walk miles in foul weather than ride in my carriage and be seen with me. According to the laws of the realm, I am an outcast. On account of me, poor Martin never felt secure on solid ground. Long ago, in Berkeley Street, he was already asking embarrassing questions. When the Emperor deserted me to marry a spotless grandee,

[1] Unpublished codicil. The Archives of Maître Mahot de La Quérantonnais.

Martin, just ten years old, resented an awful shock. He understood something terrible was going on, without exactly knowing what it was all about."

Another letter: "Martin lives in Paris and seldom comes here: yet I cannot find fault with him. The child was never happy at home. He knew my lawful wedded husband was not his father. He knew the Emperor's sons were not mine; in point of fact he actually saw them snatched from me. *Auntie Mel* [1] is no blood relative of his; when Martin discovered, all by himself, we had been telling him fibs, he sulked with us all Summer ... Now Martin, who has great expectations in diplomacy, keeps away and says I must not interfere with his plans. The Emperor is fond of him. At the reception of the *Corps Diplomatique*, both Their Majesties greeted him with a gentle smile.[2] Afterwards, during the evening, the Emperor talked with him in public, very kindly, for more than five minutes. Martin was gratified. I wish you could see him in uniform and Court breeches; he is frightfully handsome ..."

Another letter: "My son's future looks promising. Maybe I ought to live elsewhere, in England or in Italy, so as to be totally forgotten? No act of oblivion for Miss Howard as long as the Countess de Beauregard sticks to French soil! ... Martin can't help feeling I am in his way. Being on good terms with Drouyn de Lhuys,[3] he knows more than I do, and positively says my residence at Beauregard can damage his career ..."

Mrs. Trelawny, much concerned as she was for her son, still thought of the Emperor, the only man whom she had ever loved. It was with sorrow that she learnt that Napoleon III was degrading himself in a liaison with Marguerite Bellanger,[4] a *cocotte* of the utmost vulgarity, whom all Paris called " Margot la Rigoleuse." The girl was expecting a child and her Imperial protector lodged her at Saint-Cloud, in a villa next door to the conjugal

[1] Miss Melliora Findon.
[2] In the Album of the Comte de Béchevêt a photograph of the Empress Eugénie takes up a whole page.
[3] Édouard Drouyn de Lhuys (1805–81) had once more become Minister for Foreign Affairs in 1862.
[4] Justine Leboeuf, called Marguerite Bellanger (1838–86).

Palace. Elizabeth Ann was not alone in being concerned; Marguerite Bellanger's pregnancy infuriated the Empress. " This new fatherhood on the part of the Emperor," wrote Octave Aubry, " irritated Eugénie to the last extreme. She feared that the Prince Imperial's future might be prejudiced. She foresaw blackmail." [1] The angry Spaniard was beginning to regret the distant period when she had had Miss Howard for unique and only rival. " The unbelievable has happened! " wrote the Comtesse de Beauregard in 1864. " People say that, since the Bellanger entanglement and so many other scandals, the Empress herself feels grateful to me for keeping quiet all those years . . . Never does Her Majesty speak an unkind word against me . . ." [2] A small consolation amid so many sorrows! Jean Mocquard, the most faithful of friends, had died on the 12th December, regretted by all who knew him.

Prosper Mérimée to the Comtesse de Montijo, 21st December, 1864: The death of Mocquard must have much saddened the Emperor. He is very difficult to replace. In the first place, he had the confidence of a man who, I believe, does not easily grant it. Then, he had taste and tact and, on many occasions, he was most useful in modifying his master's first drafts which were sometimes extremely tendentious . . . [3]

Deprived of Mocquard, the sovereigns were thenceforward to appeal in all the complicated circumstances of their private life to his son, Amédée, lawyer to the Imperial family.

One day, the Empress announced that as " she was suffering from dyspepsia, she proposed to try a cure at the waters of Schwalbach, in the Duchy of Nassau." She left Saint-Cloud in a special train, going by the name of the Comtesse de Pierrefonds, and this sudden departure for Germany reminded informed observers of her Scottish escapade of 1860.

[1] Octave Aubry, *L'Impératrice Eugénie*, p. 200.
[2] Unpublished letters. Private collection.
[3] *Lettres de Prosper Mérimée à la comtesse de Montijo*, Vol. II, p. 262.

" What occupies serious attention now are the intestine discords in the Imperial family," wrote Lord Cowley to Lord Russell, a short time after Eugénie's return. " Le *séjour* at Compiègne has been most painful . . . The Emperor and the Empress are hardly on speaking terms. It has come to this that she taxes him with his present liaison to his face—calling the lady the scum of the earth—and he defends himself . . . One curious fact is that she has made confidants of the Walewskis, saying: ' Do not suppose that I have not always been aware *des infidélités de cet homme. J'ai tout essayé, même de le rendre jaloux. C'était pour rien*, but now that he has condescended to this *crapule*, I can stand it no longer ! . . ." [1]

Upon one occasion, the Emperor fainted at Marguerite Bellanger's. The agitated Empress ordered her carriage and asked Amédée Mocquard to accompany her to the house of this " devilish woman." The lawyer, the confidant of the sovereign, had to obey the Empress and thereby was present at a most extraordinary scene.

" Mademoiselle," said the indignant wife, " you are *killing* the Emperor! We must put an end to this. I'll pay you . . . Get out! Leave this house to-morrow morning. I repeat I'll pay you."

Lord Cowley to Lord Clarendon, 6th January, 1865: " Fancy the Empress taking Mocquard's son, a *notaire*, getting into a brougham and going off to Marguerite Bellanger to whom she made a scene, offering to settle I do not know what upon her if she would leave Paris. The offer—and the lady—were treated with the utmost contempt and the story of the bait made a good joke of."

Lord Clarendon to Lord Cowley: " Spanish blood and Spanish jealousy have often begotten imprudencies, but I never heard of such an imprudence as the visit of Eugénie to Marguerite. It was certain to end in miserable failure, as the damsel would feel sure of better provision from the husband than the wife . . ." [2]

Napoleon III considered himself seriously slighted by this

[1] *The Paris Embassy during the Second Empire*, Lord Cowley's papers, p. 273.
[2] *The Paris Embassy during the Second Empire*, Lord Cowley's papers, p. 274.

ultimatum. He lectured the Empress of the French and kept Margot la Rigoleuse. This notorious scandal made a great noise. The solitary woman at Beauregard was informed of it, as was the whole of France.

The latter's disease, incurable alas, had remained stationary for three years. Suddenly, however, alarming symptoms developed. The cancer spread; the end was near. Before dying, the patient wished to revisit the places where she had spent the most happy and prosperous time of her life. She wished to see, even if it were from a distance, the Prince Charming of her youth. During the winter of 1864–65, astonished Paris believed that Miss Howard was being rescued from the shadows. At forty-one years of age, her body had grown heavier, but her face, still angelic, retained the beauty of Reynolds's and Gainsborough's sitters. She was to be seen upon the Champs Élysées and in the Bois de Boulogne, driving her phaeton herself behind a superb pair of bay horses.

Then, at the Théâtre Italien, upon a first night to which the Emperor and Empress were going, the Comtesse de Beauregard made a supreme appearance. She had booked in advance a box in the first tier which was situated almost opposite that traditionally occupied by the Sovereigns. Long before the curtain went up, she took her place dressed " in a puce silk gown, trimmed with sable but unadorned with jewels." An English friend—was it Grant or Strode?—accompanied her. During the whole evening, leaning on her elbows upon the parapet of the box, she gazed unceasingly at the Imperial box through her opera glasses. This performance was violently criticised on the following day.

But Elizabeth had only gone there in order to watch Their Majesties from a distance. After twelve years, the Emperor, grown much older, no longer coincided with her memory of him. She had passionately loved this man whom she had lost so long ago; she knew that she was looking at him for the last time; nevertheless she had some difficulty in recognising the prince she had known and gazed without emotion upon the puffy features of what might have been a complete stranger. "His hair and face were a dirty white, his eyelids swollen, and his back bowed." He was not only a monarch weighed down by the weight of his responsibilities, by his anxiety for his country and dynasty, but he was a man exhausted by debauchery.

The beautiful Spaniard, for whom Miss Howard had in the past been sacrificed, resisted better the outrages of time. Indeed, that year, she assumed a heedlessness and a detachment which were strange to her nature. Unhappy in her married life, she encouraged young girls to marry and was bringing pressure to bear upon the prettiest princess of the Imperial blood, Anna Murat, to agree to marry Lord Granville, who was a widower and fifty years old. Lord Cowley tells (9th January, 1865) in what terms Eugénie prayed Comte Walewski to help her convince the girl who was refusing obstinately:

"But tell her," cried the Empress, "tell her that after the first night, it makes no difference whatever whether a man is good-looking or ugly, and that after a week it comes to exactly the same thing!"[1]

Eugénie's laughter sounded hollow. Her determined impassivity was no more than a mask hiding the very face of sorrow. "I am prepared to wear a mask and show a smiling face," she said, "but that is the extent of my ability. Sorrow, insomnia, madness almost, that is all that remains to me . . ."[2] The Duchess of Alba, who had died at the age of thirty-five, had, during her last illness, received sad letters from her sister. Such, for instance, as the following: "Dear Paca . . . I am so disgusted with life; the past seems so empty, the present so full of dangers, and the future perhaps so short (at least I hope so) that I frequently wonder whether it is worth fighting on? . . ." It is to be remarked that, having expressed in these terms her

---

[1] *The Paris Embassy during the Second Empire*, Lord Cowley's papers, p. 275.
[2] cf. Octave Aubry, *L'Impératrice Eugénie*, p. 200.

desire for eternal rest, the Empress Eugénie was to survive her fugitive depression for more than sixty years.

Elizabeth Ann was far from suspecting the extent of the misfortunes that had overtaken this woman, crowned with flowers and diamonds, who occupied the official box at the Théâtre Italien. The role of Empress is a difficult one and Mlle de Montijo had not known how to make a personal success of it. Would Miss Howard, surrounded with every kind of snare, abused by the pamphleteers, have filled the position better?

After this last operatic night, the Comtesse de Beauregard went back to her fantastic château. She was never to leave it again. Her last visitor was the Abbé Dubreucq, curé of Grand-Chesnay.

With the generosity of a rich woman she had supported financially the various funds of the little parish, and had for some years past been on friendly terms with the priest. She liked to talk to him of religion and, in particular, to ask him questions about the sacrament of penitence, the remission of sin, and the purification of absolution. Octavie's influence had also had some effect upon the religious evolution of her benefactress. This mystically inclined orphan wished to take the veil. Submissive, out of gratitude, to authority, she had allowed herself to be promised in marriage, but hesitated to marry her intended, praying Alfred Alderton to be patient. The conversion of Mrs. Trelawny to Roman Catholicism was, in some part at least, due to the pious girl she had chanced to give a home to at the instigation of Richard Wallace.

The Emperor was taking a cure at Vichy. In the month of July, Larrey had diagnosed the presence of a huge stone in the bladder. The whole Court was soon to be travelling to Biarritz, where Count Bismarck was to be the guest of the French sovereigns for a few days at the Villa Eugénie. Napoleon III never thought of the " hermit of Beauregard." He was told neither of her conversion nor of her illness.

Octavie d'Espinassy and Melliora Findon relieved each other throughout the twenty-four hours at the dying woman's bedside. The Abbé Dubreucq came to administer the last sacraments of the church to Elizabeth Ann Trelawny, Comtesse de Beauregard. She died on the 19th August, 1865. Her son was not present.

*   *   *

L'Indépendance belge, 22nd August, 1865:

Lady Howard (*sic*), who, barely a week ago, was driving out in her carriage and apparently in perfect health, has died if not unexpectedly at least very suddenly. She succumbed to a disease from which she had been suffering for several months . . . She will be much regretted by the poor of her parish to whom she was most liberal. Latterly, she was to be seen distributing her charity in person. Though she had become a little stouter, she was still extremely beautiful . . .

Le Temps, 24th August, 1865:

Madame la Comtesse de Beauregard (Lady Howard) died on Saturday night in her Château de Beauregard after a few days illness . . . Shortly before her death, she was converted from the Protestant religion. The Curé of Chesnay-lès-Versailles baptised her. In accordance with the last wishes of the deceased, her body will be taken to England.[1] A funeral service was held on Monday morning in the church at Chesnay. The fine property of Beauregard is left to her son . . .

Martin, an attaché at the Ministry for Foreign Affairs, lived in Paris at 17 Rue du Vert-Bois. He rushed round to Mocquard's chambers where the will was read. The main beneficiary expected to take immediate possession of his inheritance. But unexpected difficulties arose owing to the fault of the testator whose past lies even affected the title to her properties! On the 13th September, 1852, Maître Roquebert, as agent for the Baron de Guenifey, had sold the château and estate of Beauregard to " Mrs. Elizabeth Alderton, widow of Martin Haryett." The

[1] The remains of Mrs. Trelawny, Comtesse de Beauregard, were never repatriated.

usual formalities, summarised in the Deed of Sale, had taken place " in the presence of Maître Constant-Amédée Mocquard, lawyer at Provins, attorney to Mrs. Haryett, who had sworn to her identity and status."

To establish a supposititious widowhood, she had taken her mother's maiden name and invented a fictitious person called Martin Haryett senior. But, the time for play-acting was over, and this was the phase of the law. The law required that the identity of the deceased should be indubitably established before the inheritance was released.

For lack of written proof, it was necessary to call upon witnesses of unimpeachable character to give their evidence on oath. A statutory declaration was drawn up on the 13th October, 1865:

> " The following have appeared before the undersigned Maître Mocquard, attorney in Paris:
>
> (1) Baron François-Eugène-Edmond Boulart, Colonel of Artillery, Deputy-Director of Munitions, Officer of the Legion of Honour . . .
> (2) M. Émile Marguerin, Director of the Turgot Municipal School, Chevalier of the Legion of Honour . . .
>
> By these presents the above declare that they have known well Madame Elizabeth Ann Haryett, the wife of Clarence Trelawny, gentleman, who in her lifetime resided at the Château de Beauregard, in the Commune of La Celle-Saint-Cloud (Seine-et-Oise);
> And have declared by deed poll to all whom it may concern:
> That the said lady, a landowner, deceased at her Château de Beauregard on the 19th August last; that after her decease no inventory was made; and that she left as her heir, having the right to inherit:
> M. Martin Constantine Haryett, Comte de Béchevêt, her recognised natural son, domiciled at the Château de Beauregard . . ." [1]

It is to be noted, that for the first time in his life, Martin was described in a legal document as " the recognised natural son of

[1] Unpublished document from the archives of Maître Mahot de La Quérantonnais.

Elizabeth Ann Haryett." This had not been said in Mrs. Trelawny's main will.

The recognition, moreover, was purely verbal and theoretic. This was due to the fact that Mocquard, Miss Howard's lawyer, was the only government officer qualified to receive her declaration of maternity, to record it officially and, later, regularise the civil status of her son. But, in order to recognise a child legally, proof must first be made of his bastardy, that is to say the production of the birth certificate at a certain place and a certain time declaring that he is born of *unknown parents*. Mocquard did not, and could not, have in his possession any document relative to Martin's complicated origins. For lack of evidence upon which to base the recognition of a natural child, it was, in these circumstances, legally impossible for him to confirm a deed upon his own responsibility without the relevant documents.

To send to London for a copy of his certificate of baptism which, at that date in the British Isles, was equivalent to a birth certificate, was to show precisely the contrary of what had now to be proved. It must not be forgotten that in England the newly born Martin had been recorded as being a legitimate child. How, in these circumstances, could Miss Howard recognise a son who, supposedly born of a legal marriage, was therefore in no need of recognition?

From the number of beneficiaries, the main will proves her evident generosity but not her veracity for, throughout the interminable document, she persists in deception and dissimulation. For example, she makes Martin Constantine Haryett her principal legatee without ever saying that there is any relationship between herself and her chosen heir. Uncle Charles Alderton, " dear Aunt Frances " and two first cousins, Alfred and Thomas Alderton, are alone described as close relations and recognised as such.

There was a last surprise for those who thought that they knew the mysterious owner of Beauregard well. They had frequently heard the cruel and miserable story of her childhood. Harriet

Howard, as she painted herself, was a sort of martyred child whom the early death of all her family had turned into a Dickens-like character. Even the beauty of the orphan, exposed to the lust of rich and wicked men, had been the cause of her becoming a lost woman for " innocence of heart is a poor defence for a pure girl against libertines." Solitude and poverty were, she said, bad counsellors.

Her friends who had night after night heard these heartrending stories learnt with stupefaction that the parents of their hostess, supposedly dead at forty, were still living!

Mrs. Trelawny had written in her main will of 1861:

> " I give to Elizabeth Haryett, of Great Yarmouth (Norfolk), an annuity of one hundred and fifty pounds for her life, and in case her husband, Joseph Haryett, shall be living at her decease, I give to him, after her decease, an annuity of one hundred pounds during the residue of his life." [1]

It is surprising to see the testator name her own parents after her housemaid and her reader, and without mention of the family link. What does this peculiarity signify?

The strange attitude of a woman who, while dividing up her wealth, never calls the Haryetts " my parents " nor the Comte de Béchevêt " my son," can have but one explanation. The testatrix was embarrassed, paralysed by the memory of her first monumental deception. Mr. and Mrs. Haryett in more than twenty years had not raised a single protest against their daughter's lie. They had therefore remained, legally, the father and mother of their grandson.

It is clear from the holograph will of Mrs. Trelawny that when *in extremis* she did not know her parents' address. In 1865, Joseph Gawen Haryett, householder, and Mrs. Haryett, née Alderton, his wife without profession, were living in Dover on their savings. They possessed a charming little house, 13 Victoria Crescent.

[1] Unpublished. From the Archives of Maître Mahot de La Quérantonnais.

Sir Richard Wallace

Martin Harryett, son of Miss Howard

Mrs. Trelawny moreover did not know that under French law parents would jointly inherit half their daughter's estate. In Great Britain, as residual legatee, Martin would have inherited, notwithstanding the existence of a surviving father and mother. But the Code Napoléon stipulates that: "real estate situated in France, even that owned by foreigners, is controlled by French law." The English nationality of Mrs. Trelawny affected her personality and she could leave part of her liquid assets, which were in any case across the Channel, as she wished. But her estate of Beauregard in France had to be treated as a French asset. Under articles 757, 1006 and 1008 of the Civil Code, this estate would belong half to Mr. and Mrs. Haryett and half only to Martin.

The two old people suddenly learnt that their daughter had died wealthy somewhere on the Continent; that she had designated her natural son, ennobled as a Count of the French Empire, as her heir; and also that an annuity of £150 would be paid to Mrs. Haryett by the trustees.

A little later, they were invited to go to London in order to meet their grandson in the offices of William Mark Fladgate, solicitor, who, having explained the situation, proposed a compromise.

The interview took place on the 29th January, 1866. It has left traces behind it since there resulted a document of seventy-two pages, written out on stamped paper and entitled: *Agreement relative to the French real estate in joint ownership, having belonged to the late Mrs. Trelawny, Countess of Beauregard.*

This family agreement is a capital document, since everything that had been suppressed is here stated at last.

In view of the fact that the said Countess has deceased without having made a Will valid by French law;

And in view of the fact that the said Countess has left a surviving legitimate husband, Clarence Trelawny;

And in view of the fact that Martin Constantine Haryett, Count of Béchevêt, is the unique and natural son of the late said Countess, recognised in the form prescribed by the French Code;

And in view of the fact that Joseph Haryett and Elizabeth Haryett are, respectively, the father and mother surviving of the late said Countess;

—The parties concerned have been advised that, in accordance with the laws of the French Empire, the Will of the deceased Countess and the legacies therein contained of Château, lands and estate of Beauregard were (and are) ineffectual, and therefore without power to transmit the properties of which, under the French laws, the testatrix had not the right to dispose . . .

In accordance with these laws, all the real estate situated in France, which belonged to the said Countess during her life, should, at her decease, pass to the extent of two quarters to Joseph and Elizabeth Haryett, as her parents; and, of the other half undivided to the Count de Béchevêt, as the only natural and recognised son of the said Countess, as aforesaid . . .[1]

Forty successive purchases had made of Beauregard an immense estate but the deeds corresponding to each accession of land all needed revision. Amédée Mocquard attached to them a frank and true *rectification of the names of Mrs. Trelawny:*

This is to show that it is wrong and erroneous:

If Mrs. Trelawny, who was then unmarried and bore only the name and christian names here following:

Elizabeth Ann Haryett: has been described by the following names: *Mrs. Elizabeth Alderton, widow of Mr. Martin Haryett,* in the contracts dated 13th September 1852, 8th and 10th December 1852, the 16th, 18th and 23rd January 1853, et cetera, all deeds of purchase here enumerated;

And, by the same names, with the qualification: *Countess de Beauregard,* in the seven contracts of the year 1853;

And if, in the contracts of 3rd March 1859, of the 8th September 1860, of 30th March and 2nd April 1861, Mrs. Trelawny, then married, has been given the christian name of Elizabeth alone instead of Elizabeth Ann which are her real christian names . . .

Moreover, the said Mrs. Trelawny and the person thus named are identically the same . . .[2]

[1] Unpublished. The Archives of Maître Mahot de La Quérantonnais.
[2] Unpublished. The Archives of Maître Mahot de La Quérantonnais.

Martin had charm. In a few months he succeeded in winning over his astounded grandparents. This clever diplomat, whose face was moulded upon that of Little Bess, was, at twenty-four, a very fine looking young man. He attracted the girls and pleased his elders.

In order that Martin might enter into the possession and enjoyment of Beauregard without delay, Mr. and Mrs. Haryett were tactfully and respectfully invited to abandon their share. Generously, they agreed at once to do so.

The last act of the family drama took place on the 26th June, 1866, in the chambers of Maître Mocquard, who was the instrument of this renunciation. The principal participants were the lawyer, the grandfather, the grandmother and the illegitimate grandson. The secondary participants were Nathaniel Strode and Captain Lousada, who were both executors of Mrs. Trelawny's will and, as such, present as witnesses.

For those who can read between the lines and find beneath the pompous phrases of an archaic style the tragic and the human, lawyers' documents may sometimes attain to a certain grandeur. The document in which Maître Mocquard explains in precise and moderate terms the motives which persuaded the old couple, who were far from rich, to withdraw in favour of the radiant grandson, is a model of its kind. The reader may judge it from the following:

> Mr. and Mrs. Haryett, being desirous of putting into execution, wholly and completely, the last wishes of Mrs. Trelawny, their daughter, who had always manifested the intention of leaving the whole estate of Beauregard, which she had made and erected, to the Count de Béchevêt;
>
> It is thought that the simplest method of attaining this end is to make a gift to the Count de Béchevêt of the half belonging to them in French law in their capacity as heirs to their daughter.
>
> Moreover, they believe that they can make no better choice for the execution of their intentions than Messrs. Strode and Lousada, here present, who always had the confidence of Mrs.

Trelawny, and had been chosen by her as the executors of her Will . . .

In accordance with the above:

Mr. and Mrs. Haryett do by these presents and while yet alive make an irrevocable gift to Mr. Martin Constantine Haryett, Count de Béchevêt, resident at present at the Château de Beauregard, and who expressly accepts it,

Of the half they own (the other half being already the property of the co-heir, as is said above), of the estate of Beauregard and its dependencies, situated in the Commune of La Celle-Saint-Cloud, in the Arrondissement of Versailles (Seine-et-Oise), the whole being of an area of 477 acres.

Once the deed had been signed, the Haryett grandparents crossed the Channel and went home. The two ghosts had emerged out of a forgotten past only after Elizabeth Ann's death and for long enough to enrich their unknown grandson.

Riches tend to multiply. The stud of Bel-Ébat was productive of yearlings; tree-felling goes in cycles and, at Béchevêt, market-gardening had been developed with success owing to the proximity of Paris. In short, the total revenue of the estate of Beauregard averaged at that time sixty thousand gold francs (equivalent in 1956 to £12,000). The voluntary renunciation of half the property by the Haryetts is not lacking in a certain nobility. This was felt by the honest Mocquard and also by the grateful recipient, for the annual pension of the good old people was raised to seven hundred pounds a year.

The aberrations of Harriet Howard, Countess de Beauregard, had ruined her whole life. The same lies were to torment her descendants to the third generation. In the twentieth century, her grandson, Richard, second Count de Béchevêt and godson of Richard Wallace, had to bring a tiresome lawsuit in London to lay claim to his hereditary rights. In September 1907 the English newspapers were once again to pose the question of identity to Miss Howard's unquiet ghost. Never was an inheritance encumbered with more extraordinary complications.

CHAPTER THIRTEEN

AND SHALL TRELAWNY DIE . . .

ONCE MRS. TRELAWNY had been safely buried, Octavie d'Espinassy prayed her fiancé to release her from her engagement. "Christian virginity and religious celibacy are," she wrote to the good Alderton, "more seemly in the sight of God than marriage." Released from her promise, she took the veil and, still young, died in a convent.

Martin, a very considerable snob, was determined to make a brilliant marriage. It was always possible that the Faubourg Saint-Germain, too well-informed, would not accord him the hand of an aristocrat, because the prejudice against Miss Howard was still extremely strong in that intransigent society. The young diplomat only succeeded in finding the kind of fiancée he wanted abroad. The contract, which included terms regarding the dowry, was signed at Vienna on the 20th January, 1867. Then, in "the free and royal city of Posen, in the Parish of St. Martin on the 29th January, 1867," he married in great pomp Marianne Caroline Josephine von Csuzy, "an aristocratic and catholic young lady." She was the daughter of a Magyar gentleman, who was allied to the greatest families in Hungary and was Lord of Ogyalba, near Comorn. Prince Koudacheff and three Counts Esterhazy von Galantha signed the register as witnesses. In diplomatic circles, Béchevêt passed as the beloved, though illegitimate, son of the Emperor of the French. Martin gave his wife as a wedding present the diamonds which Miss Howard had worn at the opera under the Second Republic. He described the splendours of Beauregard with such eloquence that the blonde Marianne was enraptured.

When the newly married couple went to France, they took up their residence in the magnificent château. Two daughters were born there: Anne, eleven months after the marriage on 23rd December, 1867, and Giselle-Charlotte on the 28th December in the following year.[1]

Alas, time was short and Beauregard was heavily mortgaged. The owner, an inveterate gambler, had borrowed 670,000 gold francs on the estate. In the wild hope of re-establishing the situation, he made absurd speculations on the Stock Exchange. Martin, though he gave posthumous grandchildren to the Comtesse de Beauregard, dispersed the family inheritance. He was compelled to meet his debts.

In January 1870 he sold Beauregard to the Duchesse de Bauffremont. When all his debts had been paid, the prodigal possessed the sum of 784,000 gold francs. Four months later, his charming wife gave birth to a son: Richard Martin, born in Paris on the 11th May, 1870.[2] The mutual love of this good-looking couple was unhappily not to survive the reverses of fortune that arose from the destruction of the Second Empire. On the night of the 19th or 20th September, 1870, the Prussians occupied La Celle-Saint-Cloud. General Schmidt made the Château de Beauregard his headquarters. In October, a great review of the German troops was held in the park. The château, standing in its ravaged garden, was fortified to meet a *sortie* of Parisians.

When the war finished, the Comte de Béchevêt's ruin was

[1] The two sisters were married in the same year. The eldest, on 24th October, 1888, married Félix-Edmond de La Poix de Fréminville by whom she had four children. It is her eldest son, Commandant Yves de La Poix de Fréminville, who owns the portrait of the Comtesse de Beauregard by Cappelaere, and who has been kind enough to permit its reproduction in this book. The younger daughter of the Comte de Béchevêt, who married Gaëtan-Ernest-Gustave Ratisbonne de Ravenel on the 2nd December, 1888, had two children, baptised Emmanuel and Germaine.

[2] The second Comte de Béchevêt died without issue. He married Mlle Lydie de Basilevitch on the 9th February, 1909.

complete. He saw the furniture which his mother had collected with so much enthusiasm dispersed by auction.

Le Figaro, 28th February, 1872:

It was with curiosity that yesterday we visited the rooms of the Hôtel Drouot, where superb furniture will be sold to-day by order of the Official Receiver. The furniture embellished the Château de Beauregard, which was inhabited under the Empire by a foreign lady of whom there was much talk. The interest aroused by such a quantity and quality of furniture, superb Gobelins tapestries and valuable objects of every kind, can be easily imagined . . .

Beauregard had so much suffered under enemy occupation that the Duchesse de Bauffremont, since she had no available capital, gave up the idea of restoring the magnificent château; she preferred to get rid of it. On the 27th June, 1872, a Belgian financier, Baron Maurice de Hirsch, bought the whole estate for 850,000 gold francs.

Béchevêt, wholly discomfited, sought refuge in London. There, conjointly with his stepfather Trelawny, he brought an action against Nathaniel Strode to release the fortune administered by the trustee (an unrealisable trust, set up long before the marriage of Mrs. Trelawny), and make it immediately available to the two prodigals who were in urgent need of liquid cash.

Marianne de Béchevêt, who had remained in France, leased a flat in the Place Vendôme. The social newspapers of the time tell us that she was " one of the most beautiful blondes in Parisian society." *L'Événement* declared in its number of the 17th January, 1881: " The Comtesse de Béchevêt speaks every language and sings like a nightingale." She had considerable success and entertained a great deal. Both her daughters were exquisitely beautiful.

Under the Naquet law, a divorce was granted at Mantes by the Civil Courts which finally separated those whom God had joined at Posen.

In his later years, Martin reappeared in France. Without ceasing to be legally domiciled in London, he lived in Paris for some time at 18 Rue Matignon. While spending the summer at Meudon-Bellevue, he died there on the 22nd August, 1907. When his children wished to know the extent of their father's fortune in England, since he had died intestate, Gilbert Howard Terrell, who was in charge of winding-up the estate, told them that the late Comte de Béchevêt at the time of his death was in possession of exactly £45 sterling.

It is well known that Camden Place, where Napoleon III was to end his days, had been the property of the Rowles family and that he had stayed there when, as a young Pretender, he was plotting to become Emperor. Some authors add that, about 1839, there was an intended marriage between Prince Bonaparte and Miss Emily Rowles, the daughter of his hosts. But no French author has ever stated that, when Camden Place was put up for sale after the suicide of Henry Rowles and the departure of Emily, married to Marchese Campana, for Florence, the purchaser was Nathaniel Strode.[1]

Strode was the faithful friend of Miss Howard for a quarter of a century, a witness at her marriage with Trelawny, and an executor of her will. There is more than coincidence here.

As is well known, the government of the Third Republic, in order to discredit the dethroned " Badinguet," hurriedly published a detailed account of the *Expenses of the Civil List* as well as the private accounts of the Imperial family. To the list of the pensioners of the Empire were added all those who, for whatever reason, had ever received sums of money. Thus in the publication in which the Tuileries papers are quoted, we find:

STRODE (Nathaniel) received, for reasons unknown, a total sum of 900,000 francs, paid at the rate of 50,000 francs per month during the Second six months of the years 1862, 1863, 1864.

[1] Mr. Ivor Guest, who tells the story of Camden Place in his *Napoleon III in England*, tells us that Augustin Filon, tutor to the Prince Imperial, was surprised to find in this English house a portrait of Jean Mocquard. The latter must clearly have given it to Nathaniel Strode before his death.

Strode was an extremely rich man who never had any personal financial embarrassments and it is impossible not to see some form of "Harrieterie" in this matter. One knows that from 1842 he was employed to administer the inalienable personal property of Miss Howard and that he fulfilled these functions till her death. The years 1862–64 were precisely those during which Mrs. Trelawny, exploited by her husband, was faced with distressing financial difficulties. It is not impossible that Strode, who was a friend from 9 Berkeley Street days and for whom Napoleon III always preserved a considerable friendship, may have profited by a stay at Beauregard to acquaint the Emperor with the situation. It is possible that by these secret means the ex-mistress was rescued from embarrassment. His every move watched by the jealous Eugénie, the Emperor could not have sent 900,000 gold francs (£180,000 to-day) to a woman, herself at a husband's mercy, without the Empress discovering it. There were likely to be violent manifestations of her Castilian temperament. On the other hand, payments spread over a period, made from the Civil List to an honourable English financier, might have passed unperceived.

André Lefevre, commissioned in 1872 to publish the *Tableau des Subventions*, preceded by a prefatory note, mentions the ex-favourite in these terms:

> HOWARD (Miss), created Comtesse de Beauregard by the Emperor. The Commission have already published the documents establishing the huge advances that this lady made before the 2nd December . . . She received in 1853 monthly sums in repayment to the value of several millions.[1]

The same Lefevre shows farther on that Strode received 900,000 francs *for reasons unknown*. He seems not to have known that Strode was Miss Howard's man of business.

After the closing of the Universal Exhibition in Paris in 1867, the main gate was put up for sale and Strode bought it for

---

[1] *Papiers et Correspondance de la famille impériale*, Vol. II, p. 141.

Camden Place. This monumental gate ornamented the entrance to the property down to recent times. But when, during the last war, the English government demanded the collection of iron, it was removed and melted down.

Eugénie de Montijo and Harriet Howard, who had vied against each other for the love of an inconstant man, had a certain number of solid friendships in common.

When, on the Sunday after Sedan, the Empress-Regent left the Tuileries in the middle of an insurrection, she took a cab to the house of Dr. Evans from whom she hoped for help and protection. This was the same dentist to whom, in 1849, the Prince-President had not dared send his mistress, for fear that Miss Howard's reputation should be compromised if she were seen entering his house. Napoleon III's legitimate wife, upon whom the temporary duty had been laid of governing the French Empire, showed no such scruples of propriety when, on the 4th September, 1870, she boldly took refuge with Thomas Evans. Revolution makes cowards of us all.

It is well known that the dentist arranged the Empress's flight. He took her to Deauville, where she was able to hide on the *Gazelle*, a racing yacht belonging to Sir John Burgoyne. The schooner set sail at dawn. The Empress landed at Ryde in the Isle of Wight, from where she went to Brighton.

The Emperor, prisoner at Wilhelmshöhe, received tender letters from his wife: " Dearest friend," she wrote on the 30th January, 1871, " to-day is the anniversary of our wedding . . . I want to tell you that I am very fond of you. In good times, the links between us may have grown loose. I had thought them broken, but stormy days have shown me how solid they are and, now more than ever, I am reminded of the words of the evangelist: ' for richer, for poorer, in sickness and in health, to love, cherish, and to obey . . .' " [1]

When Napoleon III rejoined his exiled wife in England, he found her installed at Camden Place, which Strode had placed at

[1] *Lettres familières de l'Impératrice Eugénie*, Vol. II, p. 202.

their disposal for the duration of their exile. Not being in the habit of *letting* his house, he insisted on offering his hospitality to the fallen sovereigns.

For some time, Camden Place sheltered under its roof and at its table a simulacrum of the French Court, the master of the household and an artist without commissions, Guillaume Fodor, who was, also, a permanent guest of the kindly Strode. Mrs. Trelawny had left the poor devil an annuity of forty pounds a year in her will.

However, Strode discreetly put Cranmore Lodge, a smaller house of his, in order and, so that the unfortunate sovereigns should feel really at home in Camden Place, went to live there with Fodor. The latter, shortly afterwards, was killed in a carriage accident on the Eltham road. Thus the first annuity under the will lapsed.

Nathaniel Strode was fifty-five when, on the 6th July, 1872, he married Miss Eleanor Courtney. Napoleon III, by now gravely ill and with only six months to live, nevertheless made the journey to London to act as witness to his host and sign the marriage register at All Saints Church in the parish of St. Margaret's Westminster. It was at Camden Place, Chislehurst, that the Emperor of the French died on the 9th January, 1873. The Empress, realising that her exile was permanent, insisted on paying a rent even if it were only token. Strode leased her his huge place for £200 a year. The lease, with their two signatures appended, is displayed at Camden Place (now the clubhouse of the Chislehurst Golf Course) in the drawing-room where, successively lying in state, the coffin of Napoleon III was followed by that of his unfortunate son, the Prince Imperial, who was killed in Zululand in 1879.

The Empress lived at Camden Place for seven years as a widow. She never suspected that Strode, in offering asylum to Napoleon III and his family, believed he was obeying " a compulsion from above." Strode thought, as did the elder Dumas, that Harriet had loved her *Poléon* as ardently as Desdemona loved

171

Othello,[1] and that it was one of the great love stories of the century. In inviting the deposed Emperor to Camden Place, Strode thought that he was acting in conformity with the will of the dead woman whose last wishes he had been entrusted to carry out, *all* her last wishes. Had she not, when living, offered asylum to the man she had so much loved?

Upon the Sunday after the disaster, the Empress-Regent, threatened with death by a raging mob, had owed her safety to Dr. Evans. Then Strode had sheltered her in his own country house, and she stayed there ten years. Evans and Strode? . . . Two friends of the woman she had execrated.

*   *   *

What, in the meantime, had happened to Trelawny?

In the first place, there is a brief answer to this question in the memoirs of Lady Cardigan:

" Clarence Trelawny was a friend of mine, and the poor fellow came to a sad end. After his wife's death, he married an American lady, but unfortunately he got into debt. He appealed to his relations, who were very wealthy but apparently equally mean, for they refused to lend him the £400 he asked for, and driven desperate by worry he blew out his brains . . ." [2]

More recently, the sad history has been related by Mr. W. H. Holden:

" The Comtesse de Beauregard had been a very beautiful woman, but her former husband seems to have decided resolutely to forget her very existence. Five years after her death, on the 15th November, 1870, Clarence Trelawny married another striking beauty. His second wife was Miss Mary Campbell, daughter of Mr. W. S. Campbell, the United States Consul at Dresden. By her he had five daughters, and remarkable and incredible though it seems, he contrived for twenty years to keep his wife and children in complete ignorance of his former marriage . . ." [3]

[1] cf. Albert D. Vandam, *Undercurrents of the Second Empire*, p. 112.
[2] Countess of Cardigan and Lancaster, *My Recollections*, pp. 102-3.
[3] W. H. Holden, *The Tragedy of Clarence Trelawny*, pp. 55-6.

The curiosity of Eve does not seem to have been among Mary Campbell's faults. When, in Dresden, she gave her hand to a good-looking Englishman, this man of forty-four declared himself to be the widower of the first Mrs. Trelawny, née Harriett, long dead in foreign parts, and without any children born of the marriage. Neither in America, nor in Germany, had the Campbell family heard speak of Miss Howard, the forgotten mistress of an exiled sovereign.

In 1890 Rose Trelawny, the eldest daughter of Clarence and Mary, was proposed to by Count Bathyani, an officer of the Radetzky Hussars. In this Austrian regiment, in which Trelawny had himself once served, his first marriage had made too much noise not to be recalled upon the occasion of the Bathyani-Trelawny engagement.

When, in the theatre to-day, we hear Father Duval saying to Marguerite Gautier, the Lady of the Camellias, that the engagement of his beloved daughter will be broken off if her fiancé's family get to know that her brother has a courtesan as mistress, we tend to laugh and say that the scene lacks verisimilitude! This, nevertheless, is what happened to the innocent Rose Trelawny. Count Bathyani refused to give his name to a girl whose father had dared to marry legally " a professional beauty " after a historic scandal. It was all the more unjust since Rose was *not* the daughter of Miss Howard. The word of God: " I ... visit the sins of the fathers upon the children," should work out its terrible results only in the direct line.

Mr. Holden, having decided to write *The Tragedy of Clarence Trelawny*, obtained abundant documentation from two surviving daughters of his hero: Lady Stanton Woods and Miss May Trelawny. He gives the following account of the suicide:

" Trelawny had unfortunately always been extravagant and luxurious ... Although never in serious financial straits, as time went on he underwent temporary difficulties; he lived up to, and beyond, his income, and always rejected advice to economise, saying that he was ' too old to retrench.' "

Trelawny was seventy-six when the crisis came. At that time he was living at 9 Denzil Avenue, Southampton. On the 27th November, 1902, he took the train to Reading. His presence in that town has never been explained. Perhaps, originally, he had the intention of visiting his son-in-law, Captain Liebert, who lived at Fernacres Farm, near Fulmer. Instead of going there, he took a cab and drove to the Royal Berkshire Hospital. While the cabby was asking for some information from the hospital porter, Trelawny, armed with a pistol, fired a bullet into his head. He lingered throughout the night.

An inquest was held. A letter put in as evidence gives the explanation of a long premeditated act. Before killing himself, Clarence Trelawny had written to his solicitor, Mr. Lupton. His lack of resources which, he said, had been tormenting him for the last seven years, no longer allowed him to live in even decent retirement. Since he was also the victim of an incurable disease, he preferred to take the desperate course of putting an end to himself at once. He ended the letter in these terms:

" This is a terrible letter to write, but there is no escape for me . . ." [1] The jury brought in a verdict of " suicide during temporary insanity."

Clarence Trelawny fell a victim to the disease of money.

[1] W. H. Holden, *The Tragedy of Clarence Trelawny*, pp. 56-7.

CHAPTER FOURTEEN

BAGATELLE

RICHARD SEYMOUR-CONWAY, fourth Marquess of Hertford, had only survived his friend Elizabeth Ann by five years. During the latter part of his life, the cunning man had plotted a secret and underhand method of detaching large sums of money from the entail upon his estates. His huge revenues, drawn from England, were transferred to France and invested in real estate, pictures and *objets d'art*, and these escaped the English laws of inheritance.

Lord Hertford, a bachelor, had never told any members of his family of his intentions. Nor had he admitted that he was the father of the young man who lived under his roof and resembled him as a son might have done. Richard Wallace, brought up by Lady Hertford, called his grandmother " Aunt Mie-mie," but no one ever heard him address his father otherwise than as " Sir."

As the estate consisted of a fortune estimated at three million pounds, General Francis Seymour, the heir and future fifth Marquess of Hertford, was naturally somewhat concerned about his distant relative's affairs. Victor Seymour, the General's son, and several other lesser Seymours had an eye on the huge unentailed fortune. They plied the aged collector with attentions and politeness. To amuse himself, the latter encouraged their expectations and talked to them in such a way that they had great hopes.

Lord Hertford's will was deposited neither with an English

175

solicitor nor with a Parisian *notaire*. For the last nineteen years it had been locked up in the drawer of an old desk in London. When his strength began to decline, the Marquess curtly ordered Wallace to leave for England and bring back the table in question. Since he was given no explanation, Richard thought that it was a mere caprice of the patient's. The desk was brought to Bagatelle and placed in his room where, from his four-poster bed, the lover of rare pictures could gaze upon Gainsborough's " Perdita."

About this time, Sir Hamilton Seymour visited the head of the family. The latter, seriously ill, was confined to his room. In the presence of his relation, he opened the locked drawer of the table, drew out a thick envelope sealed in several places, and gravely said: " This will interest you, Hamilton! "

On another occasion, Lord Orford was touched to hear the old man cry: " One's family is everything! Remember that . . . No man who belongs to a great family has the right, whatever his feelings may be, to despoil it by leaving part of his property to strangers! " The Seymours were delighted with these admirable sentiments! Richard Wallace, alone, was never told anything of the Marquess's will. The latter never spoke of it to his inseparable companion.

In Paris, both the Court and the town thought that the Prince Imperial would be the heir to Bagatelle. While still quite small, the latter used to go and play in the beautiful park and ride in the stretch of land between the château and the Seine. When Napoleon III had expressed the wish to buy the terrestrial paradise for his son since the child was passionately fond of it, Lord Hertford had excused himself, saying that " His Majesty had no need to spend the money, since Monseigneur was *chez lui* at Bagatelle." The Imperial family had immediately come to the conclusion that the delightful estate would be left to the heir to the throne.

When the war of 1870 broke out, the Prince Imperial, leaving for the Front at the age of fourteen, paid a good-bye visit to

Lady Wallace, née Julie Castelnau

Miss Howard's Tomb at Grand Chesnay

Lord Hertford. The Empress accompanied her son. She nervously reiterated: " It was written ... To Berlin! To Berlin! " She was a warmonger for reasons of prestige and because the Emperor was becoming unpopular. Could France, after the Mexican disaster and Sadowa show herself subject to the wishes of Prussia? Eugénie believed that only a victorious war could give the dynasty back its complete authority. At Bagatelle, the Empress declared that a lightning campaign would cut Germany in two while the Prussians were still mobilising. When the two august visitors had left, the sick man said to Richard Wallace: " Poor France! Poor Paris! Poor little Prince! This woman is about to plunge us all into the abyss! "

Colonel Claremont, military attaché at the British Embassy, and Sir Edward Blount, his two most intimate friends, came to Lord Hertford's bedside. Since the news from the front was bad, they wished to send the dying man across the channel, but it was impossible; he would not have been able to bear the fatigues of the journey. They found Mrs. George Idle at his bedside and, naturally, Richard Wallace. The Marquess did not know them and died while they were yet there.

When the will was made known, there was consternation among the Seymours. Everything had been left to Richard Wallace! The fifth Marquess would only inherit the houses in Suffolk and Warwickshire, which were entailed, but none of the fortune which would have allowed him to maintain them. The less important Seymours were disinherited. To Mrs. Idle and Mlle Bréart the will gave annuities in exact proportion to the number of years they had lived in sin with him.

Thus Amelia Idle, in her seventies, acquired an income of twelve thousand pounds a year. She died in 1879. The White Lady, Louise Bréart, twenty years her junior, was allowed only two thousand pounds a year, but enjoyed them till 1902. Miss Adèle Gurwood who, in her childhood, knew her well, says that " in spite of her story and the character of the man she had lived with for so many years, she was curiously prim and rigid in her ideas."

Lord Hertford, who had failed to marry Agnes Wallace, the mother of his son, or Mrs. George Idle, the widow of his friend, or Louise Bréart, a talented woman, had always opposed a marriage between Richard Wallace and Julie Castelnau. Besides his natural hostility to marriage, Lord Hertford had three complaints against her: he resented her ill-temper, her lack of elegance and her stupidity.

When, towards 1860, Richard had had an affair with Apollonie Sabatier (the " Présidente " dear to Baudelaire) [1] and had housed the beauty at Neuilly, in order that she might be close to Bagatelle, Lord Hertford had hoped for the dismissal of the insufferable Julie. But Richard was not the man to dismiss the mother of his only child. He deceived her because the flesh is weak and, having seen la Femme au Serpent by Clésinger, a statue for which Mme Sabatier had posed entirely naked, he had dreamed of her beautiful body while in the bed of an ugly woman, who had never allowed him to sleep in a separate room and gloried in it.

Capable of infidelity, Wallace nevertheless considered the annulment of an unwritten contract of marriage, after twenty-four years of life together, to be a monstrous disloyalty. He refused to commit so vile an action which, moreover, the " Présidente " had not asked of him. The sculptural Apollonie was simply carrying on her profession of demi-mondaine. To replace the Belgian, Alfred Mosselman, by the Englishman, Richard Wallace, was merely moving from Montmartre to Neuilly; from an entre-sol in the Rue Frochot to a private house in the Rue de Chézy. The " woman with the serpent " merely wanted a house with a garden, not a sacrifice in the manner of Corneille.

Though she could excite Richard sensually, she could not warm his exacting heart. The fire of straw soon left nothing

[1] Aglaé-Joséphine Savatier, called Apollonie Sabatier (1822–89).

but cold ash. On his way from Paris to Bagatelle, the honest man ceased going round by Neuilly.

In 1870 Richard Wallace, who for a month had been in possession of his father's huge fortune, learnt that Apollonie, an improvident creature, was ruined. He took action at once.

> *Journal d'Edmond de Goncourt:* Flaubert tells me of the unhoped for good luck of the Présidente (Mme Sabatier, the *Femme au petit chien* of whom Ricard has done so admirable a portrait), who has received a deed for fifty thousand francs a year, two days before the siege of Paris; it was sent by Richard Wallace, who slept with her in the past . . .[1]

* * *

While Lord Hertford was alive, Julie Castelnau had never suggested marriage. But, after the patriarch's death, she never ceased asking Richard Wallace to marry her day and night. Should not their son, then thirty years old, be legitimised at last?

A Frenchman, born in Paris of an unmarried French mother, Edmond Richard had become a professional soldier. He had reached the rank of captain when war was declared and distinguished himself under General Vinoy, who was in command of the XIIIth Army Corps.

Bagatelle had been requisitioned and fortified. A battery of artillery had replaced the flowering orange trees on the terrace. Richard Wallace remained in Paris where, during the whole of that terrible year, he did an enormous amount of good. Already the founder of an ambulance unit, which followed the troops to the front, he created two hospitals in the town, one for wounded soldiers and the other for sick civilians. The Government, together with the diplomatic corps, had departed along the road which, three wars in succession, was to be that of defeat:

---

[1] *Journal des Goncourt,* Vol. IV, p. 354.

Paris–Tours–Bordeaux. Lord Lyons[1] went with them with the whole staff of the British Embassy. There were, nevertheless, two thousand English shut up in Paris during the siege. Only one official remained to look after them: Sir Edward Blount, who had temporarily been made Consul.

When food ran short, Richard Wallace decided to feed those of his fellow-countrymen who no longer had money to buy it, the price of the exiguous foodstuffs having become prohibitive. His charities that year cost him 2,500,000 gold francs (half a million pounds sterling to-day). It was at this time that he was nicknamed *Providence des pauvres*. Francisque Sarcey later dedicated to him in moving and eulogistic terms his book entitled: *Le Siège de Paris*.

The famished town surrendered on the 28th January, 1871. Between the surrender of Paris in 1871 and the Commune, Julie Castelnau triumphed. In the British Consulate, before Sir Edward Blount, Richard Wallace married his elderly mistress. The lugubrious wedding of a fifty-two-year old bride.

Louise Bréart had so often told the story, both at Beauregard and Bagatelle, of the drama of her youth that Julie was invincibly suspicious of every form of English marriage. Was this friend of Lord Hertford, Consul merely by accident, more qualified than a false clergyman to unite two lovers in the name of the law? Concerned for the validity of their union, Julie, barely married, wished to be remarried before the Mayor of the district in which she had been domiciled for the last thirty-two years. Wallace consented. For the banns which had to be posted in the Rue Drouot, he stated his particulars as follows: " Richard Wallace, landed proprietor, born in London on the 26th July, 1818, domiciled at 3 Rue Taitbout, Paris."

With his usual bashfulness, he refused to name his parents. His mistress proudly stated that she was " of independent means; born in Paris on the 15th March, 1819, of the legal marriage of

---

[1] Lord Cowley, having spent fifteen years as British Ambassador in Paris, had been allowed to resign in July 1867. Lord Lyons had succeeded him.

Bernard Castelnau with Sophie Knoth." The ceremony took place on the 15th February, 1871.

After the Commune and the burning of palaces, Wallace, who had never suffered from physical fear, was afraid that his collection, the object of his passionate devotion, might be in danger. Paris had risen four times in a single century. Civil war had just destroyed Saint-Cloud, the Tuileries, and the Cour des Comptes. The inheritor of the treasures accumulated by his father at Bagatelle and in a variety of houses situated in the Rue Lafitte, the Boulevard des Italiens and the Rue Taitbout, Wallace thought it his duty to remove so many wonderful things from the dangers of insurrection and revolution. In July 1871 he had Hertford House, Manchester Square, prepared to receive the most famous items of the collection.

He had lived in France for forty-seven years. In order to make his own country attractive to him, Her Majesty's Government decided to honour him. Although illegitimate, was he not half Seymour and half Wallace? He was made a baronet and given the Order of the Bath for his philanthropy. He had just founded, at Levallois-Perret, the Hertford Hospital for the sick English of Paris.

Elected to Parliament for Lisburn, he took up his residence in his constituency and built there a house which is the exact replica of Hertford House. But Bagatelle remained his favourite place of residence; he still spent a month or two there each year.

Though a rich man, Wallace was not a happy one. His unexpected inheritance, his honours, and the House of Commons could none of them give him domestic happiness. Fat Julie was discontented and sulked. She did not like England and bitterly criticised every decision her husband made. Transplantation bewildered the middle-aged woman who was a slave to her habits. In her youth, Lady Wallace had been a child of Bohemia in the Mürger manner. It did not predispose her to play the part of a great lady in England. Disagreeable in Paris, she became odious in London.

Victorian society which, twenty years earlier, had treated Mrs. Trelawny as a pariah, nevertheless received Lady Wallace kindly. She was accepted exactly as any woman of good family and irreproachable morals would have been.

Marcel Proust would have delighted to analyse the mysterious forces by which two women, whose destinies had followed such similar paths, were treated in such unjustly different ways. Lady Wallace and Mrs. Trelawny both belonged by birth to the lower classes. They were born in the same period, Julie in 1819, Little Bess in 1823. They had both had natural sons before they were of age. Julie Castelnau was vulgar; Harriet Howard, tactful and of considerable distinction. Until the time of her late marriage (that is to say up to the age of fifty-two), Mlle Castelnau had lived publicly as a kept woman; at twenty-three, Miss Howard had become faithful and disinterested. Why did Lady Wallace benefit by a plenary indulgence, while the interdict against Mrs. Trelawny was never lifted? Society has reasons that the reason cannot know.

When Lady Wallace, either in London or in her country houses, had to live up to her rank, she let it be seen that she was " bored to death." The obligation she was under to entertain and, as she said, to " feed too many people," wounded her innate meanness. To show people round the galleries at Hertford House was intolerable drudgery to her.

In November 1872 Lord Cranbrook noted, during a week-end at Sudbourn Hall: " The dinner was good, too good, and required care and firmness. Lady Wallace speaks only French ... I took her in, to my dismay, and stumbled through some very bad language."[1] At fat Julie's, she saw to it that one did oneself well. She might have made an admirable housewife in circumstances better adapted to the extreme simplicity of her tastes. Lady Wallace only admired " women who could do their own cooking and sewing." She had such a horror of society that for fifteen years she pretended to know no English, merely because

[1] Quoted by Bernard Falk in *Old Q's Daughter*, p. 274.

she did not care to be obliged to take part in the conversation at her own table. Nevertheless, she openly read the *Morning Post*. Lady Wallace's silences, her corpulence and her immobility made of her a sort of female Buddha. But when her exasperated guests lost the habit of treating her as a living being, she took exception: " You are the first of my guests, Monsieur, who has been so good as to address a word to me," she said to a Frenchman who paid his respects to her during a big reception at Hertford House.

" Lady Wallace's presence was rather springing a mine on one," wrote Lady Wolseley after a dinner-party. " Harmless and dowdy, she refuses to speak a word of English. But Sir Richard is charming . . ." [1]

Henry Reeve paints the collector in the following terms: " The very type of gentleman of the highest breeding—rather stern, melancholy, not at all humorous, and incapable of vulgarity or pretence . . ." [2] Everyone was sorry for this obliging and elegant man who had married so ill.

The Prince of Wales (later King Edward VII) was a friend of Richard Wallace for twenty years. When he went to spend a few days at Sudbourn Hall during the shooting season, his hostess was invariably indisposed . . . She took a certain pleasure in arranging a table laden with plate and gleaming crystal, but she could not bear the thought of having to sit on His Royal Highness's left and get herself into difficulties when addressing him in the third person.

Lady Wallace wore the rivière of diamonds which had belonged to Catherine Parr (the sixth and last wife of Henry VIII) who, having married a Seymour after the King's death, had brought the jewels into the family. But, seeing the dead Queen's collar round fat Julie's throat, hearing her sighs of victimisation, one might have thought that, laden with chains, a rope already

---

[1] *The letters of Lord and Lady Wolseley.*
[2] Quoted by Bernard Falk in *Old Q's Daughter*, p. 283.

about her neck, she was being dragged to the scaffold by an executioner.

The life at Sudbourn Hall, with its pleasures and its mishaps, emerges clearly from the charming letters that a French guest, the Comte d'Armaillé, wrote to his family from England. Here are a few extracts:

The Comte d'Armaillé to his daughter, the Princesse de Broglie, 17th *November,* 1878: There is a change of plan in prospect, my dear Pauline. The Prince of Wales has lost a member of his family and is not coming ... Poor Wallace has spent huge sums of money in order to entertain the Prince. Sudbourn has been newly decorated. He has had extremely beautiful curtains made at Lyons ... All the liveries are new. Lady Wallace admitted to me that her dresses were "foolish." The rooms which they had arranged for the Prince are truly royal; the bedroom and dressing-room were still in the Paris Exhibition a fortnight ago. And all this for nothing! [1]

The following year, fortunately, no Court mourning interrupted the Prince's shooting, which was a success.

Sudbourn Hall, Wickham Market, 16th *November,* 1879: We arrived here, my dear Célestine,[2] after a very pleasant little journey. There are two triumphal arches and the whole front of the house is decked with flags; there are poles surmounted with the Prince of Wales's feathers and quantities of bunting ... The Prince arrives to-morrow in time for dinner with a numerous suite and we shall shoot from Tuesday to Friday.

I found Wallace much changed and much weaker; he believes himself to be very ill and is much affected by it. The Marquis de Malterre is to come and spend the week with Victor and Pauline.[3]

Monday, 17th: The Prince arrives to-night and we shall shoot to-morrow ... Lady Wallace was ill yesterday and remained in bed ... I hope she will be better by this evening, because

---

[1] From an unpublished letter in the Archives of the Comtesse Jean de Pange, née Broglie, granddaughter of the Comte d'Armaillé.

[2] The Comtesse Louis d'Armaillé, née Célestine de Ségur.

[3] The Prince and Princesse de Broglie, who had been invited to Sudbourn Hall and were to arrive a few days later.

it would be most disagreeable if she were unable to greet the Prince . . .

19*th November*, 1879: I have just received your letter as I came in from shooting, my dear Célestine. Yesterday we shot approximately six hundred head; to-day, between seven and eight hundred, but we have walked a long way through bracken and furze and I am exhausted . . . Wallace is delighted that Victor and my daughter are coming; he will do everything in his power to entertain them. There are few partridges, but much other kinds of game. Victor will never have seen anything of the sort and I shall be delighted to see his pleasure in it . . .

21*st November*, 1879: The Prince of Wales has left for London . . . Lady Wallace, who was better yesterday, is very ill again to-day and talks of going to London to be properly looked after. If she is not better to-morrow morning, I will send you a wire to stop them coming . . . Victor will have to counter-order the cabin . . . If you receive no wire from me, it will mean to say that Lady Wallace is better and that they can start . . .

Saturday: I hope, my dear Célestine, that you will have received the wire in time to stop the poor children setting out. Lady Wallace spent a bad night . . . Wallace seems to me to have lost his head and, this morning, came to ask me to prevent their leaving . . . I have very much enjoyed myself this last week; but I am exhausted, and sick with annoyance at being obliged to stop the children at the moment they were leaving!

Sunday, 23rd November, 1879: Wallace is in a highly nervous state . . . The week has exhausted him, for he organised the shoot the whole time. I have just been out for a walk with him; he was complaining all the time. We went to see his wife, whom I had not seen since Friday night. She was in a dressing-gown on her chaise-longue . . .[1]

Such were Julie's caprices.

*　　　　*　　　　*

In the same year as his marriage, Sir Richard had taken on a bilingual secretary, John Murray Scott. The son of an English

[1] Unpublished letters from the Comte to the Comtesse d'Armaillé kindly placed at my disposal by their granddaughter, the Comtesse Jean de Pange.

doctor practising at Boulogne-sur-Mer, which was then a fashionable seaside resort, the young Scott had gone into the insurance business from which Wallace one day extracted him. Clever, active, and intelligent, he was also appreciated for his evident professional qualities. He became friends with his master and was taken fully into his confidence. As for Lady Wallace, she conceived a senile passion for the boy of twenty-four which was to have important consequences. Since she no longer loved her husband and had never loved her son, Scott became the unique object of her affection.

The private secretary succeeded in making himself indispensable to this ill-assorted couple. He played an incomparably subtle game between the gouty old man and the complaining old lady. He never contradicted the unhappy pair. His secret weapon was flattery.

Edmond Wallace was not pleased to see a complete stranger take so important a place in his father's house. Since he frequently showed the intruder his dislike of him, he quickly made of Scott an enemy.

Genes and chromosomes make the individual an odd mixture of inherited characteristics. Edmond was at once both like his father and his mother. His honesty, his physical courage and his loyalty to his word were characteristics inherited from Sir Richard. His stubbornness, roughness and lack of social sense came from Julie Castelnau.

Captain Wallace who had sent in his papers after the Commune, was only happy in Paris, in the Bohemian circle in which he had lived with a young woman called Amélie-Suzanne Gall by whom he had had four children. He lived in idleness upon an allowance from his father and was very much a family man. Once a year, he went to England to shoot, but it bored him. The ceremonial formality of social life irritated the unamiable man.

In 1876 Sir Richard advised him to become a naturalised Englishman. Unsuited to politics himself, the Baronet nevertheless hoped to see his son succeed him as a member of Parliament and take root in Lisburn. "Monsieur Edmond" would one day be Sir Edmund Wallace, provided that he changed his nationality. Much occupied with social reform, Sir Richard wanted to improve the lot of his labourers and foresters who, from generation to generation, created the wealth of the ancestral estate. Edmond would dedicate himself to this noble task.

A more delicate matter was that his father particularly desired him to marry according to his own views. To marry a Seymour, Sir Richard said, was to be grafted on to the elder branch. It would also mean bringing back to Lisburn a descendant of the dispossessed heirs, thus repairing the injustice that had been done to the profit of the bastard branch. Edmond replied that "his honour and his affection forbade him to leave the mother of his children." It was precisely in these terms that forty years earlier Richard Wallace had replied to Lord Hertford, when the latter had taken it into his head to set Julie Castelnau aside. But Sir Richard, having become old, had changed in his behaviour. Having for so long played the part of son, he now played that of an authoritarian father. The form and subject of family dramas do not change from generation to generation.

At first Lady Wallace encouraged Edmond's revolt. It pleased her to see a young man attached to his little family, totally indifferent to the fact that he belonged to a great line. Suddenly, under the influence of Scott, Julie changed sides and took Sir Richard's part against her only child. Relations soon became strained.

"Sir Richard had sketched out an ambitious future for his son," writes Bernard Falk. "Only complete estrangement could end such prolonged bickerings. It is not necessary to disentangle from the past the exact circumstances of the quarrel, destined, alas! to work out to the grievous disadvantage of the innocent grand-children ... On the one side was the desire to establish a line of English landed proprietors who should carry on the Wallace name;

on the other, the desire to live his own kind of life and maintain such intimacies as seemed good to him. Less obstinate and quick tempered men would have found ways and means of adjusting their differences, but as this was not to be, each went his way, and dreed his weird . . ." [1]

They were never reconciled.

*   *   *

Sir Richard, when he knew that he was failing, briefly put down his last wishes in the form of a draft. These were intended to be properly formulated when he had consulted competent lawyers. In this document, he left all his worldly wealth " to my dear wife " and charged her with the obligation of pensioning off their faithful servants generously. The private secretary, John Murray Scott, was to receive twenty thousand pounds for twenty years of devoted service.

Long before he had received his fantastic inheritance, Richard Wallace, as a young man, had invested his early savings in the purchase of an old house, called the Bains Chinois, which was situated in the Boulevard des Italiens. In one of its flats he had at that time lodged Julie Castelnau and his little son. Tender, distant memories undoubtedly inspired him with the choice of the only legacy he made Edmond, who had been lost to sight for ten years but to whom, by his order, a Parisian bank paid a handsome allowance.

Wallace junior never knew that he was to inherit 29 Boulevard des Italiens, for, upon the 14th March, 1887, the rebellious son died at the age of forty-seven, three years before his father, in a flat he had leased at 25 Avenue Marceau, near the Étoile. He was not placed in the pyramidal, Egyptian-style Mausoleum in which reposed his great-grandmother, third Marchioness of Hertford, his grandfather, fourth Marquess, his great-uncle, Lord Henry Seymour, and where already a niche had been prepared beneath the coffin of *Milord L'Arsouille* to receive the

[1] Bernard Falk, *Old Q's Daughter*, p. 273.

mortal remains of Sir Richard Wallace, K.B., first Baronet of the bastard branch.

Edmond, the disreputable deceased, found a place somewhat farther off in Père-Lachaise, in the tomb of his great-aunt, the Marquise de Chevigné, née Frances Seymour (1798–1822). His premature death left four orphans, all born and brought up in France, of whom the eldest was nearly fifteen.[1] The attitude of Sir Richard and Lady Wallace, who obstinately refused to see their grandchildren, was much criticised at the time. Scott was beginning to be suspected of bringing undue influence to bear on the matter of the will.

Five weeks before his death, the great collector summoned to Bagatelle a French notary and an English solicitor. They talked of the proposed will, but the condition of the sick man became so rapidly worse that a second meeting could not be held. The previous dispositions, hastily drafted before Edmond's death, had to be adhered to. They were to make of Lady Wallace an all-powerful widow and a fabulously rich woman.

On the 20th July, 1890, Sir Richard died in the room in which Charles X had slept and Lord Hertford had died before him. The letter announcing his death, preserved by the Prince and Princesse de Broglie, has been placed at my disposal by their daughter.

The implacable Julie refused to allow the names of her grandchildren to be printed, as was the custom, below her own.

Lady Wallace was then seventy-one years of age. Her stubbornness and insensitiveness remained unaltered.

John Murray Scott, her constant companion, had placed other members of the Scott family about her; she was flattered, hedged about and protected from all interference from the outside world—" sequestrated," said Sir Richard's old friends.

The draft will under which she was the beneficiary said nothing

---

[1] Marie-Richard-Georges Wallace (1872–1941), was a Brigadier-General, a Commander of the Legion of Honour, and won the Croix de Guerre in the 1914–18 war, having been nine times mentioned in despatches.

M

Lady WALLACE

A l'honneur de vous faire part de la perte douloureuse

qu'elle vient d'éprouver en la personne de

Sir Richard WALLACE, Barᵗ K. C. B.

son Epoux, décédé le 20 Juillet 1890, en son Château de Bagatelle

(Bois-de-Boulogne), à l'âge de 72 ans.

Trois choses demeurent :
La Foi, l'Espérance et la Charité ;
Mais la meilleure est la Charité.

Saint-Paul.

Règlement des Convois, ROBLOT, place du Louvre, rue de la Pompe-Passy, 80, rue Drouot, 7, rue de Bretagne, 57 et rue St-Marc 22

as to what was to happen to the collection after her death. Sir Richard had put no restrictive clause to the wholesale legacy he had made his " dear wife." He had never expressed any wish that the marvellous things collected by his father and himself should be put on perpetual exhibition to the public and handed over, for all time, to the government of a great country. Lady Wallace was completely at liberty to dispose of the collection as she pleased. John Murray Scott might, therefore, have good reason to hope.

He was clever enough to realise that he could not decently appropriate the whole of so colossal a fortune, and that the spectacular legacy of the collection to the British nation (a legacy acquired at his instigation and through his offices) would procure him the gratitude of official England. Thus he might garner all the rest of the inheritance without criticism. And, what was more, as keeper for life of the treasures of Hertford House, he could make a career for himself in the world of art and become a person of note, respected by his contemporaries. It was an ingenious plan that held promise of a splendid future.

Fat Julie had never been able to refuse her husband's secretary anything. When Scott advised her to make her will, she did so. The collection was left to the British nation.

When Lady Wallace died, full of years, on the 15th February, 1897, it was learned that her residuary legatee, John Murray Scott, inherited a personal estate of more than a million pounds; Sudbourn Hall in England, Lisburn in Ireland; Brancas-Lauraguais House and two houses situated at the corner of the Rue Taitbout and the great *boulevards* in Paris; and the little house and beautiful park of Bagatelle in the Bois de Boulogne. To her direct descendants, the dead woman had left nothing more than the house previously destined for Edmond, the Bains Chinois.

Parisian friends of Scott's then told him that, in accordance with the law which had applied to the successors of Mrs. Trelawny, Comtesse de Beauregard, the natural heirs of Lady

Wallace would have the right to half her property situated in France. Scott replied that the testatrix had scrupulously obeyed the intentions of her dead husband . . . It is certain that the collector would have fully approved the legacy of the collection, made by a Frenchwoman to her husband's country. But had Wallace really wanted his secretary to succeed, after Julie, to Lisburn, Sudbourn and Bagatelle?

The question was never posed in this form. The four grand-children, helpless, intimidated and ill-informed, did not invoke in time the articles of the civil code which would have been in their favour and, during a hasty settlement of the estate, signed all the documents placed before them. Scott acquired the huge inheritance. In 1899 he appeared in the Honours List. Already keeper of the Wallace Collection, the new Baronet was made a trustee of the National Gallery and, in 1908, received the Order of the Bath. It all came to pass as if Richard Wallace's titles and dignities must of necessity fall to the lot of his widow's irregularly chosen heir.

*   *   *

Sir Richard was not, as he had wished to be, the founder of a line of landowners in the United Kingdom, but this Englishman did found, though without premeditation, a French family of soldiers. It will be remembered that his only son had dis-tinguished himself in the war of 1870. In 1912 the elder of his grandsons [1] was a captain in the 22nd Dragoons in garrison at Rheims. This officer gained distinction during the First World War. Gravely wounded on the 5th May, 1917, he was men-tioned in the Orders of the First Colonial Army Corps. It was the ninth time that George Wallace had been mentioned in dispatches. He was promoted Brigadier-General and Com-mander of the Legion of Honour. His brother, Henry-Richard,

---

[1] This was the future General Wallace, born in Paris on the 2nd May, 1872, died at Arcachon (Gironde) on the 19th January, 1941. The three daughters born of his marriage with Mlle Gabrielle Klein, and all three surviving, are: Odette (Mme Jacques Pol-Roger), Jacqueline (Mme Georges Vernes), and Nicole (Mme Guy Schyler).

was wounded and received the Cross of a Chevalier of the Order.

The youngest of the three sons whom Amélie-Suzanne Gall gave Edmond Wallace [1] was a Lieutenant of the Reserve when he was mobilised in 1914. On the 28th February, 1915, during the attack on Vauquois where his regiment, the 89th Infantry, was decimated, he was killed at point blank range by a bullet in the head. In the margin of the death certificate of Sir Richard Wallace's grandson, is written: " Died for France."

The fourth child of Edmond Wallace was a daughter, born at Vésinet on 8th June, 1878, and baptised Georgette. Gifted with a contralto voice, she studied singing and, under the pseudonym of Lucy Arbell, made a career for herself at the Opéra in Paris. The composer Massenet,[2] who greatly admired her, engaged her to take the leads in his last operas: *Ariane*, *Thérèse*, *Bacchus* and *Don Quichotte* (in the part of Dulcinée).[3]

The future General Wallace was still only a captain of Dragoons when he published an open letter in the *New York Herald* accusing Scott " of having used every means in his power to prevent a reconciliation between Lady Wallace and her grandchildren." It was the precise truth, but Scott had not had to bring any pressure to bear to persuade his benefactress to dispossess her natural heirs. Lady Wallace had no more maternal instinct than she had hair. She wore a black wig and cursed Edmond's race. George Wallace's open letter to the *New York Herald*, reproduced in the English and French Press of the time, caused a considerable sensation. There was much talk but no redistribution of the inheritance resulted from it. Lady Wallace had had an un-merited success.

For the last time let us compare the two youthful friends: Miss Howard was twenty-three when she gave herself to Prince Louis Napoleon for life; she never ceased to love him; when he

---

[1] Edmond-Georges-Richard Wallace, born at Saint-Maur-des-Fossés on the 4th October, 1876, was killed in action at Vauquois (Meuse) on the 28th February, 1915.
[2] Jules Massenet (1842–1912), composer of *Hérodiade*, *Manon*, *Werther*, *Thaïs*, *Sapho*, *le Jongleur de Notre-Dame*.
[3] Lucy Arbell died at a house she owned at Bougival on the 20th May, 1947.

abandoned her, it was upon his orders that she made a purely formal marriage. Julie Castelnau, prudently faithful to Wallace during their long pre-marriage liaison, preferred to him a young man as soon as he had married her. Miss Howard risked everything she possessed on a *coup d'état*. Lady Wallace ended by leaving her lover her husband's fortune. Of these two unmarried mothers, one treated her son with immense generosity; the other despoiled her son's children in order to enrich her secretary. Nevertheless, to-day, no one remembers Elizabeth Ann, while Julie's name is glorified in Manchester Square.

When Mrs. Trelawny died in obscurity, she had already been in retirement from Parisian life for ten years; her burial in a village cemetery passed unnoticed. But on the gate of Hertford House, an inscription reminds the passer-by that this house full of wonders exists by virtue of a legacy made to the English nation by Julie-Amélie-Charlotte, Lady Wallace. Inside the museum, in the Founder's Hall, a bust by Charles Lebourg idealises and ennobles the giver ... Mrs. Trelawny died somewhat the poorer. Lady Wallace, at the end of her life, possessed a collection famous throughout the world, and whose present value runs into millions. England, justly grateful, honours and perpetuates her memory.

Little Bess wished to create an establishment where young fallen women might learn a trade. But this legacy was inoperative because of the all-inclusive legacy to her son. Martin was not the man to deprive himself of a single pleasure to assure the teaching of a trade to stray sheep. He preferred to ruin himself by gambling. And this is why there is no charitable foundation bearing the name of Elizabeth Ann Trelawny, Comtesse de Beauregard. The shade of Lady Wallace reigns over Hertford House, Bagatelle is scheduled as an ancient monument, Lisburn is a technical school. But all the houses where " the woman who made an Emperor " lived have been destroyed, one after the other. At Brighton, the exact position of Gerrards Court, where she was born, is not agreed. In London, her house in

Berkeley Street was demolished in 1935. In Paris, Baron Gustave de Rothschild, wishing to build a palace in the Champs Élysées, bought, in about 1885, the little house and big garden that Miss Howard had leased at the period she was still in favour. The imposing structure he built there [1] has its principal entrance at 23 Avenue Marigny and an approach from the Rue du Cirque; " Harriet's folly " has disappeared. Beauregard is still standing, but the house is decaying and foundering.

Only a mediocre actress, Miss Howard had never had the triumphs of Mlle George nor the success of Lola Montès. The mistress of the head of the State, she never played the political role of a Marquise de Pompadour, the maker and breaker of ministers. A romantic woman, she has not even enjoyed the posthumous glory of her contemporary, Marie Duplessis, whom we have seen live on under the name of Marguerite Gautier. In order to survive in the world's memory, it is better to be called the Lady of the Camellias than the Comtesse de Beauregard.

Peace to the ashes of a dead, forgotten woman, who was a great lover and an admirable mother.

[1] To-day the house belongs to Baron Alain de Rothschild, the grandson of Baron Gustave, its builder.

HISTORY AND LEGEND

AT THE beginning of the twentieth century there lived at Boulogne-sur-Mer an octogenarian who, it was said, had been in his youth Napoleon III's valet. He was probably the only Frenchman for whom, thirty-five years after Sedan, the defeated and dethroned Emperor was still the " man of providence."

When people expressed their surprise that he had never taken the trouble to have himself placed upon the Electoral Roll, the old man would attribute his political inertia to the fact that, in a Republican country, no candidates were put forward whom he felt inclined to support. It was impossible for him to " vote Bonapartist." In his little lodgings might be seen upon the walls a whole gallery of the Second Empire: lithographs of the official portraits of the Emperor; crude representations of " The Escape from the Fortress of Ham " or of " The Battle of Solferino." The place of honour on the mantelpiece was dominated by a plush frame enclosing the photograph " cabinet size " of a portrait: the picture of a woman on a horse in a long flowing habit. When on the 15th August, and again on All Saints' Day, he placed two vases each side of the portrait filled with geraniums or chrysanthemums, the neighbours said: " Old Léon is decorating the Empress Eugénie with flowers . . ." Their remarks were never contradicted; but it is true that with the years Old Léon had become very deaf.

In 1905, John Fraser, a young Scotsman, was preparing a thesis on *The Official Visits of Queen Victoria to Louis-Philippe and*

Napoleon III. He wanted to visit the Château d'Eu, and then, in spite of the incendiarism of the Communards, to make a pilgrimage to Saint-Cloud. Disembarking at Boulogne, he paused there to visit the man who was believed to be " the surviving personal servant of the last Emperor of the French," and whom visitors to the town, which was much affected by the English middle-class, had assured him was indeed so. His holiday-making friends humorously described Old Léon's habits and his worship of the Bonapartes. Naturally enough, Fraser had come to the conclusion that he was worth a visit.

The conversation was not easy. Fraser spoke French well but, the old man being stone deaf, he had to ask his questions in writing. The old man was honest enough to destroy the legend himself: he had never belonged to the domestic staff of the Palace. His much-regretted mistress, the beautiful woman on horseback, was not the Empress Eugénie. Indeed, he had only worn the green livery at the Château de Beauregard. First engaged as a footman in 1854, he had been promoted in the usual way. After eleven years of service, M. Duboz, the steward, thinking him worthy of a more confidential post, had made him assistant Keeper of the Plate. This promotion had made him assistant (with the probability of succession) to Ambroise Lesieur, Chief Keeper of the Plate, who was responsible for all the gold and silver services and the great centrepieces. Alas, the sad death of Milady had put a term to this flourishing career. The young Comte, her son, an unsatisfactory master, had come to power, reduced the household, and sent packing all the *protégés* that a kindly benefactress had for so long treated so well at Beauregard.

Fraser, while in France, was limiting his researches to the political visits of Queen Victoria; he was not the least interested in the history of a mistress. Nevertheless, he hoped to acquire from the memory of an eye-witness some factual details upon the physical appearance of Napoleon III and, in particular, upon the Germano-Swiss accent of which the Emperor, so it was said, had never been able to rid himself. Upon a piece of paper he wrote:

" To judge from the pictures upon your walls, you appear to venerate the memory of the Emperor Napoleon III. I imagine that you knew him well? "

" Ah," replied Old Léon, " I see they still talk a lot of nonsense about poor Milady! It's all lies . . . I give you my word, Monsieur, that in my time, the Emperor never came to Beauregard. I spent twelve years in the house; I never saw him there once."

Then with the inexhaustible loquacity of the deaf who are inclined to reminisce, he went on: " Many wicked things are said about Madame la Comtesse. I promise you that she was a most respectable person and fairy-godmother to the district! She spent much time with her flowers. She spent much time making music and doing tapestry work. For ten years, you can say that she hardly ever went out, and we entertained very little. Such guests as we had were fashionable Englishmen and a few artists . . . Oh, indeed, one knows very well—after all it is a matter of history—that Lady Howard, as a girl, had been seduced and that she had had, by the Emperor, M. le Comte Martin. But, if she sinned, it was most certainly because they were intending to marry . . . Wicked people succeeded in separating them and Madame la Comtesse was very unhappy. But I promise you that she passed the whole of her life in atoning for the sin of her youth . . . It was generally said that the Empress was very jealous of the past. It was in order not to anger his wife and not to further compromise Milady, that the Emperor never came to see us at the Château.

" But she, poor woman, loving him so much, always hoped for a reconciliation with them so that she might receive their Majesties in her house! It was said that she only married in order to bring this about . . . Just imagine, Monsieur, that on the ground floor of the Château there was what was known as the State Bedroom with a white marble bath. No one, and this is absolute fact, *no one* ever slept there. As far as I am concerned I believe Milady had created the most beautiful apartment she could for the Emperor ... He never came. It was a pity, wasn't it?

" Milady made all her household learn the history of the two great Napoleons. In order that we should take kindly to study, she gave us superb books and ordered me to read them aloud while the others were attending to the plate or the china. In this way, we learnt much ... And that's not all: in our little servants' rooms there were portraits of the Emperor, of Queen Hortense, of the Empress Josephine and of other Princes of the family in gilded frames. These were not just furniture, but presents that the kind lady gave us! ... All the fine things you can see here, Monsieur, were given to me by her: they came from Beauregard.

" I entered Milady's service in '54, when she was restoring the house. Yes, in those days, we said ' Milady '; it was only when she fell out with her husband that we received the order to say, ' Madame la Comtesse.' The master was addressed as ' Seur ' not ' Milord ' ... one had to say: ' Yesseur ... Noseur ... and Geste a minute Seur ...' The children (I mean the three young gentlemen who were the Emperor's sons), called him: ' Seury ' ..."

Then Fraser wrote upon another piece of paper: " What sort of a man was Mr. Trelawny? "

Old Léon replied at length: " A very difficult gentleman, Monsieur. He never said much, except when he was drunk, but when he was drunk, oh, goodness me, how he roared! ... He used to threaten M. le Comte Martin with his riding-whip and said that we should all be damned ... I never saw him except in riding-breeches or in evening clothes because at our house, Monsieur, we always dressed for dinner, even when the master and mistress were alone ... I shall never forget Milady descending the stairs in the Château on the tick of seven in a great crinoline and wearing all her pearls. Ah, Monsieur, how beautiful she was! She was like a Queen or the Virgin Mary herself, like in the picture in the *Mystères Glorieux* ... And

with all that she was goodness itself. She never blamed anyone
unjustly; on the contrary, she always had a kind word for
everyone. We were happy in service there. The village people
adored her; she wanted to be godmother to all their babies;
and she looked after the old people too ... That was the
woman, Monsieur, whom our Emperor ought to have married:
not that Spaniard! ... Because, you see, I can't rid myself of
the idea that the Empress is a woman who brings bad luck ...
Didn't they all come to a sad end? Her sister in the first place,
who died quite young and not even in her own bed: travelling,
in an hotel ... Then the Emperor: when he lost the war and
his position, he died of sorrow, that man did ... And then the
poor Prince Imperial who went and got himself killed at the
other end of the world, where the savages murdered him ...
And in spite of all that, the Empress, at more than eighty years
of age, cruises in her yacht[1] and, when in Paris, walks in the
Tuileries gardens, picking roses! I'm telling you: she's got the
evil eye and is a heartless woman."

*   *   *

Perhaps it was not altogether out of place to conclude the
story of Elizabeth Ann Trelawny, Comtesse de Beauregard, with
this ingenuous evidence from an old servant. The woman of
whom, forty years after her death, Old Léon still spoke with
enthusiasm was not the " courtesan " depicted by Fleury, nor
the " intriguer " imagined by Viel-Castel, nor " the favourite "
seen by Tocqueville, nor the " creature " that the Princesse
Mathilde lashed with her contempt ... She was a woman
purified by solitude and devoted to the remembrance of her
lost love.

It was only just that premature death should have spared her
the triple sorrow of seeing the Emperor defeated, the Empire
abolished, and the Château de Beauregard sold by her son.

[1] The Empress Eugénie died on the 11th July, 1920, in her ninety-fifth year.

BIBLIOGRAPHY

MANUSCRIPTS

Unpublished Letters of Elizabeth Ann Haryett, Comtesse de Beauregard, Mrs. Trelawny, to several correspondents. Private collection

Archives of Maître Jacques Mahot de La Quérantonnais, greatgrandson and successor of Maître Amédée Mocquard, notary to the Imperial family

Archives of Mme la Comtesse Jean de Pange, née Princesse Pauline de Broglie

Ministère de la Guerre, état-major de l'armée: Historical Archives

Parochial Register of the Church of Saint Nicholas at Brighton (formerly Brigthelmstone) now transferred to the Church of Saint Peter, built only in 1824

Parochial Register of Holy Trinity Church, Marylebone, London

Parochial Register of Saint James's Church, Westminster, London

PUBLISHED MATERIAL

ALMÉRAS, HENRI D', *La Vie Parisienne sous le Second Empire*. Paris, Albin Michel, 1933

ANON (Pseudonym of JULIAN OSGOOD FIELD), *Uncensored Recollections*. London, Eveleigh Nash & Grayson, 1924

— *More Uncensored Recollections*. London, Eveleigh Nash & Grayson, 1926

— *Things I shouldn't tell*. London, Eveleigh Nash & Grayson, 1924

APPONYI, COMTE RODOLPHE, *Journal du comte Rodolphe Apponyi*. Published by Ernest Daudet, 4 vols. Paris, Plon, 1913–26

AUBRY, OCTAVE, *Napoléon III*. Paris, Fayard, 1929

— *L'Impératrice Eugénie*. Paris, Fayard, 1931

— *Le Second Empire*. Paris, Fayard, 1938

BIBLIOGRAPHY

AUGUSTIN-THIERRY, A., *La Princesse Mathilde*. Paris, Albin Michel, 1950

— *Son élégance le duc de Morny*. Paris, Amiot-Dumont, 1951

BARROT, ODILON, *Mémoires posthumes d'Odilon Barrot*. Vol. III. Paris, Charpentier, 1876

BERTAUT, JULES, *Amours tendres et tragiques*. Paris, Amiot-Dumont, 1952

BILLY, ANDRÉ, *La Présidente et ses amis*. Paris, Flammarion, 1945

BOULENGER, MARCEL, *Le Duc de Morny*. Paris, Hachette, 1925

BROTONNE, LÉONCE DE, *Les Bonaparte et leurs alliances*. Paris, Honore Champion, 1901

CAMP, MAXIME DU, *Souvenirs d'un demi-siècle*. 2 vols. Paris, Hachette, 1949

CARDIGAN AND LANCASTER, COUNTESS OF, *My recollections*. London, Eveleigh Nash, 1909

CASTELLANE, MARÉCHAL DE, *Journal du maréchal de Castellane*. 5 vols. Paris, Plon, 1895–97

CASTILLON DU PERRON, MARGUERITE, *La Princesse Mathilde*. Paris, Amiot-Dumont, 1953

CHEETHAM, F.-H., *Louis Napoleon and the genesis of the Second Empire*. London, John Lane, The Bodley Head, 1909

CLARETIE, JULES, *L'Empire, les Bonaparte et la Cour*. Paris, E. Dentu, 1871

COLOMBIER, MARIE, *Mémoires. Fin d'empire*. Preface by Armand Silvestre. Paris, Flammarion, no date

COWLEY, EARL, *The Paris Embassy during the Second Empire*, from the papers of Henry Richard Charles Wellesley, first Earl Cowley, edited by his son, Colonel the Honourable F.-A. Wellesley. London, Thornton Butterworth, 1928

DANSETTE, ADRIEN, *Les Amours de Napoléon III*. Paris, Fayard, 1938

DECAUX, ALAIN, *La Castiglione, dame de coeur de l'Europe*. Paris, Amiot-Dumont, 1953

DESTERNES, S., and CHANDET, H., *La Vie privée de l'impératrice Eugénie*. Paris, Hachette, 1955

EUGÉNIE, L'IMPÉRATRICE, *Lettres familières de l'Impératrice Eugénie*. Published by the Duke of Alba with the help of F. de Llanos y

Torriglia and Pierre Josserand. Preface by Gabriel Hanotaux, 2 vols. Paris, Le Divan, 1935

EVANS, THOMAS W., *Mémoires du docteur Thomas W. Evans*. Translated by E. Philippi. Paris, Plon, 1910

FALK, BERNARD, *Old Q's daughter, a strange family history*. London, Hutchinson, 1951

FLEISCHMANN, HECTOR, *Napoléon III et les femmes, d'après les mémoires des contemporains, les pamphlets, les journaux satiriques, des documents nouveaux et inédits*. Paris, Bibliothèque des Curieux, 1913

FLEURY, GÉNÉRAL COMTE, *Souvenirs du général comte Fleury*. 2 vols. Paris, Plon, 1897–98

FLEURY, COMTE and SONOLET, LOUIS, *La Société du Second Empire*. 4 vols. Paris, Albin Michel, no date

FOUQUIER, MARCEL, *Jours heureux d'autrefois*. Paris, Albin Michel, 1941

FRAVATON, M., *Le Chateau de Beauregard*, article published in the *Revue de l'Histoire de Versailles et de Seine-et-Oise*, 12th year, No. 1. Versailles, Librairie Léon Bernard, 1910

GAYOT, ANDRÉ, *François Guizot et Madame Laure de Gasparin*. Paris, Bernard Grasset, 1934

GONCOURT, EDMOND and JULES DE, *Journal*. *Mémoires de la vie littéraire*. 9 vols. Paris, Charpentier, 1887–96

GRAMONT, ÉLISABETH DE, DUCHESSE DE CLERMONT-TONNERRE, *Le Comte d'Orsay et Lady Blessington*. Preface by André Maurois. Paris, Hachette, 1955

GUEST, IVOR, *Napoleon III in England*. London, British Technical and General Press, 1952

HOLDEN, W. H., *The Tragedy of Clarence Trelawny*. Chapter III of *They Startled Grandfather*. London, British Technical and General Press, 1950

HOUSSAYE, ARSÈNE, *Les Confessions*. *Souvenirs d'un demi-siècle*. 6 vols. Paris, E. Dentu, 1885–91

LOLIÉE, FRÉDÉRIC, *Les Femmes du Second Empire*. *La Cour des Tuileries*. *Les Grandes Dames de Compiègne*. 2 vols. Paris, Bibliothèque Historia, Éditions Jules Tallandier, 1954

LACRETELLE, PIERRE DE, *Secrets et Malheurs de la reine Hortense*. Paris, Hachette, 1936

LA FAYE, JACQUES DE, *La Princesse Mathilde*. Paris, Émile-Paul, 1928

LESLIE, SHANE, *The Letters of Mrs. Fitzherbert and connected papers.* London, Hollis and Carter, 1944

MAUPAS, M. DE, *Mémoires sur le Second Empire, par M. de Maupas, ancien ministre.* 2 vols. Paris, E. Dentu, 1884–85

MENIÈRE, PROSPER, *Journal du docteur Prosper Menière.* Published by his son, Dr. E. Menière, preceded by a biography by Dr. Fiessinger. Paris, Plon, 1903

MÉRIMÉE, PROSPER, *Correspondance générale*, edited and annotated by Maurice Parturier, with the collaboration of Pierre Josserand and Jean Mallion, 9 vols. Paris, Le Divan, 1941–47, for volumes I to VI, and Toulouse, Edouard Privat, 1953–55, for Volumes VII and IX

— *Lettres de Prosper Mérimée à la comtesse de Montijo.* Published by the Duke of Alba. Preface by Gabriel Hanotaux, 2 vols. Paris, published privately, 1930. Edition of 500 copies not for sale.

NAUROY, CHARLES, *Les Secrets des Bonaparte.* Paris, Émile Boullion, 1889

Notes and Queries, a medium of intercommunication for literary men. Eleventh series, Vol. IV, July–December 1911. London, published at the Office, Bream's Buildings, by John C. Francis and J. Edward Francis

ORANO, COMTE D', *La Vie passionnante du comte Walewski, fils de Napoleon.* Paris, Les Éditions Comtales, 1953

Papiers et Correspondance de la famille impériale. 3 vols. Paris, Imprimerie Nationale, 1870–72

PERSIGNY, DUC DE, *Mémoires du duc de Persigny.* Published by H. de Laire, comte d'Espagny. Paris, Librairie Plon, 1896

RÉVÉREND, VICOMTE A., Editor of the *Annuaire de la noblesse de France: Titres et Confirmations de titres. Monarchie de Juillet. Seconde République. Second Empire. Troisième République, 1830–1908.* Volume XI of the *Inventaire des Archives du Sceau de France.* Paris, Honoré Champion, 1909

RIMINI, BARON DE, *Mémoires de Griscelli de Vezzani, dit le baron de Rimini.* Brussels, Imprimerie Ch. and A. Vanderauvera, no date

SACKVILLE-WEST, VICTORIA, *Pepita.* London, The Hogarth Press, 1937

SAINT-HÉLIER, LADY, *Memories of Fifty Years.* London, Edward Arnold, 1910

STERN, JEAN, *Lord Seymour, dit Milord l'Arsouille.* Paris-Geneva, La Palatine, 1954

TASCHER DE LA PAGERIE, COMTESSE STÉPHANIE DE, *Mon séjour aux Tuileries, 1852–1858.* Paris, Paul Ollendorff, 1893

THIRRIA, H., *Napoléon III avant l'Empire.* 2 vols. Paris, Plon, 1895

TOCQUEVILLE, ALEXIS DE, *Souvenirs d'Alexis de Tocqueville,* with an introduction by Luc Monnier. Paris, Gallimard, 1942

TREICH, LÉON, *Les Alcôves de Napoléon III.* Paris, Éditions des Deux Sirènes, 1948

VANDAM, ALBERT D., *Undercurrents of the Second Empire.* London, William Heinemann, 1897

VICTORIA, QUEEN, *The Letters of Queen Victoria.* Edited by Arthur Christopher Benson and Viscount Esher. 3 vols. London, John Murray, 1908

VIEL-CASTEL, COMTE HORACE DE, *Mémoires sur le règne de Napoléon III.* 6 vols. Berne, Imprimerie Haller, and at all the bookshops, 1883–84

VIZETELLY, E.-A., *The Court of the Tuileries, by "Le Petit Homme Rouge."* London, Chatto & Windus, 1907

WAKE, JOAN, *The Brudenells of Deene.* London, Cassell, 1954

Wallace Collection Catalogues, Introduction to the Fifteenth Edition of the (Short account of the scope of the Collection). London, 1928. Printed by His Majesty's Stationery Office. Crown Copyright reserved

INDEX

i

A NOTE ON THE TYPE

THE TEXT of this book has been set on the Monotype in a type face named Bembo. The roman is a copy of a letter cut for the celebrated Venetian printer Aldus Manutius by Francesco Griffo, and first used in Cardinal Bembo's *De Aetna* of 1495—hence the name of the revival. Griffo's type is now generally recognized, thanks to the researches of Mr. Stanley Morison, to be the first of the old face group of types. The companion italic is an adaptation of a chancery script type designed by the Roman calligrapher and printer Lodovico degli Arrighi, called Vincentino, and used by him during the 1520's.

PRINTED *by The Murray Printing Company, Forge Village,* *Massachusetts.* BOUND *by H. Wolff, New York.*

Date Due